Modern Hungarian Driving

Preface 5	

**Breeds Suitable for Coaching
and for Driving Events** 7
Putting Together a Hungarian Team 7
The Choice of Horses 7
The Arab 11
The Lipizaner 13
The Nonius 13
The Hungarian Half-Bred 15
The Trotter and its Cross-Breeds 16

**Hungarian Carriages
and the Marathon Vehicle** 17
**Style Carriages Used
for Dressage and Presentation** 17
**Cross-Country Carriages Used
for the Marathon** 21
Axles 22
Wheels 23
Suspension 24
Fifth Wheel 24
Swingle-Trees 24
Pole 24
Coach-Box 25
Brakes 25
Other Fittings 25

Hungarian Harnesses 29
Parts and Function of a Hungarian Harness 30
Breast-Band 30
Shoulder-Strap or Withers-Strap 31
Back-Strap with Pommel and Girth 31
Traces 34
Bridle 35
Leading Reins 36
Crupper 38
Neck-Strap 38
Bearing Rein and Connecting Strap 39
Harness Decorations 40
Studding and Bells 42
The Most Popular Hungarian Harnesses .. 43
"Cseklész" Harness 43
Harness with Metal Studs 44
Light Hungarian Ceremonial Harness with
Decorative Studding 44
Heavy Hungarian Ceremonial Harness with
Decorative Studding 45
Hungarian Ceremonial Harness with Fretwork
Decoration 45
"Pozsony" Harness 46
"Jukker" Harness 46
Draught Harness 47
Adjusting the Harness to the Horse 47

The Driver's and the Groom's Dress   49

The Technique of Hungarian Driving   55
**The Proper Method of Holding and Using
the Reins and the Whip** 55
The Basic Grip 55
The Actuating Grip 55
The Basic Grip with the Whip in One's Hand   55
Shortening the Reins 57
Lengthening the Reins 57
Using the Reins when Turning 57
Backing the Team 58
Starting the Team 59
Halting the Team 59
Changing Pace and Gait 59
Using the Whip 59
Training Team Horses 60
How to Prepare a Team for Competitions   61
Presentation and Dressage 61
Cross-Country Driving or the Marathon ... 64
Obstacle Driving 70

Score Sheets 73

LÁSZLÓ TÓTH   Modern Hungarian Driving

CORVINA

Translation by Gabriella Glaser
Translation revised by Charles Coutts
Drawings by Ferenc Seeger

Design by Julianna Rácz

Photographs by:
Nándor Hajba (1, 2, 4, 6, 7, 8, 9, 11, 15, 17, 18, 20, 22, 23, 25, 26, 27, 28, 30, 31, 32, 33, 34, 35, 37, 38, 39, 40, 43, 47, 48, 49, 50, 51, 52, 54, 55, 57, 58, 60, 62, 63, 64, 66, 67, 68, 69, 70, 71, 76, 77, 79, 80, 81, 82, 83, 84, 85, 86, 87, 92, 94, 95, 96, 98, 99, 100, 101, 104, 107, 108, 112)
Zoltán Kölcsényi (12, 14, 24, 29, 34, 36, 42, 44, 46, 53, 56, 59, 61, 65, 72, 73, 75, 78, 88, 89, 90, 91. 102, 103, 105, 106, 109, 110, 111, 113)
Vera Kövesd (3, 5, 10, 13, 16, 19, 21, 45, 97)
Dr. István Mészáros (41, 74)
Gábor Váradi (93)
Cover photos: Tibor Hortobágyi, Zoltán Kölcsényi

1 Rustic carriages on Equestrian Days in Hortobágy

© László Tóth
ISBN 963 13 2673 X

Preface

In the nineteenth century, and even at the beginning of the twentieth, a great variety of horse-drawn vehicles, such as stage-coaches, drags, hansom cabs, hackney carriages, mail-coaches, peasant carts and wagons could be seen on the town and country roads of Hungary. This colourful world of the carriage as part of everyday life has disappeared in inverse ratio to the rapid advance of motorization. Stage and mail-coaches are no longer seen on our roads. Hackney carriages and cabs are only tourist attractions. However, the horse-drawn vehicle has survived on household and auxiliary farms, in agricultural co-operatives and forestries. An increasing number of horses are kept for sport and recreation. Equestrian sports have made remarkable progress during the last few decades and their popularity has increased in our motorized world. One of the newest of the equestrian sports, carriage-driving, has recently been accorded official recognition.

The International Equestrian Federation adopted a resolution in 1970 concerning four-in-hand World and European Championships: a World Championship every two years, in the even years, a European Championship in the odd years. Continental carriage-and-pair championships were also initiated, beginning in 1983. At all these events Hungarian drivers have consistently achieved excellent results as can be seen from the table of results at the end of this book. The Hungarian equestrian world was forever honoured by the fact that Budapest was the venue of the first European Driving Championship.

Driving a four-in-hand is definitely not an inexpensive amusement, and the cost restricts the number of those who can take part in it. More people can participate in the somewhat less costly carriage-and-pair events with a chance of being selected later for a four-in-hand.

In some scientific circles the invention of the carriage is attributed to nomadic peoples acting under the force of necessity. Others contend that the vehicle was the invention of ancient civilizations, and the debate on this issue remains to be settled. However, it is a fact that the ancestors of the Hungarian people did already know and use carts and carriages at the time of the conquest and settlement of the area of Hungary in the ninth and tenth centuries.

The first historical mention of wheelwrights

2 Rustic three-horse carriage from the Alföld

3 The most popular Hungarian yoke harness

4 Rustic carriages in Apajpuszta

is in the AD 1001 Foundation Deed of the Abbey of Pannonhalma. The first record of cartwrights is in the charter of Pécsvárad. These two documents prove that coach-building is an old, traditional Hungarian profession. From the eleventh century onwards innumerable other extant relics—objects, writings—confirm this statement.

Developments in breeding and in other equestrian activities were brutally interrupted by the Second World War. Horses which survived the war could only be used in agriculture. Today an increasing number of horses are being kept for sport and entertainment in which their probable future is to be found. There are a considerable number of horses suitable for drawing carriages.

In order to be successful in carriage driving a detailed knowledge of the sport is essential. This book seeks to be a guide to those who are already pursuing this activity, as well as to those who wish to make a closer acquaintance of the sport.

The main supporters of Hungarian tradition in carriage-driving are the drivers themselves; the judges at events also play an important role. This book will, therefore, present the sport of carriage-driving based on the methods of successful Hungarian drivers who have always tried to preserve true tradition.

In conclusion, I would like to express my thanks to all those who have assisted me in gathering material for this book.

THE AUTHOR

Breeds Suitable for Coaching and for Driving Events

Putting Together a Hungarian Team

The Hungarian carriage-driving tradition is still alive in many agricultural co-operatives and state farms. In the absence of books on the subject, carriage-driving knowledge has been passed on orally from generation to generation and by the practical use of accumulated experience: many of the old skills have survived intact, though time has often allowed distortions to creep in.

While taking into consideration Hungarian tradition and the requirements of the officially recognized equestrian events, we shall present the necessary aspects of equipping a team.

Besides the traction power of coaching—the horses—other accessories such as harness, vehicle and its fittings are of vital importance. In selecting them, care must be taken regarding harmony, since vehicles should not only meet the demands of practicability, but also those of aesthetics. Unfortunately mistakes often occur, when practicability is given preference and proper appearance is neglected. There are examples of the opposite as well: coaches overdecorated but not at all practical.

One can draw on a great variety of possibilities when fielding and equipping teams in Hungary. Nevertheless, the examples we shall quote here should not be allowed to lead to uniformity. It would be unfortunate to obscure this colourful world.

The Choice of Horses

Horses bred in Hungary have been formed by the demands of everyday life. But not all of the available breeds fully meet the requirements for driving events. This is a natural fact, as they have not been bred for this purpose.

Carriage-driving as a competitive sport does not have a long history. Since the first European Championship in 1971 not even two decades have passed. Such a short time in horse breeding means that we cannot even speak about an individual breed especially suitable for driving competitions.

However, experience gained so far at interna-

5 Dog-cart (single-horse vehicle)

6 Rustic carriage-and-pair from Hajdúszoboszló

7 The ancient Hungarian harnessing method: two horses with breast harness hitched to a wagon from Hajdúszoboszló

8 Rustic three-horse carriage from the area around Debrecen

9 Popular four-in-hand with the driver seated on the coach-box. Hortobágy, 1983

10 Popular five-horse carriage driven from the saddle

11 Rustic seven-horse carriage driven from the saddle. Hortobágy, 1983. The ancient Hungarian harnessing method: with no more than two rows of horses. A carriage drawn by two rows of horses had sufficient room on the wide roads of the Hungarian Plain

tional events and in Hungary do give breeders, team-owners and drivers some guidance as to which breeds will produce a competitive team. In this book we shall deal exclusively with Hungarian breeds, especially with those breeds which have already proved in events a capacity to meet the criteria of modern harness competition.

Initially appearance determined the composition of a team, and this remains the main criterion of choice of the most suitable animals. Matching size and colour are of utmost importance. A given breed almost offers the necessary matching characteristics for basic team formation, so that only movements, temperament and willingness remain to be considered. Although it would be a mistake to believe that four horses of the same breed and size produce

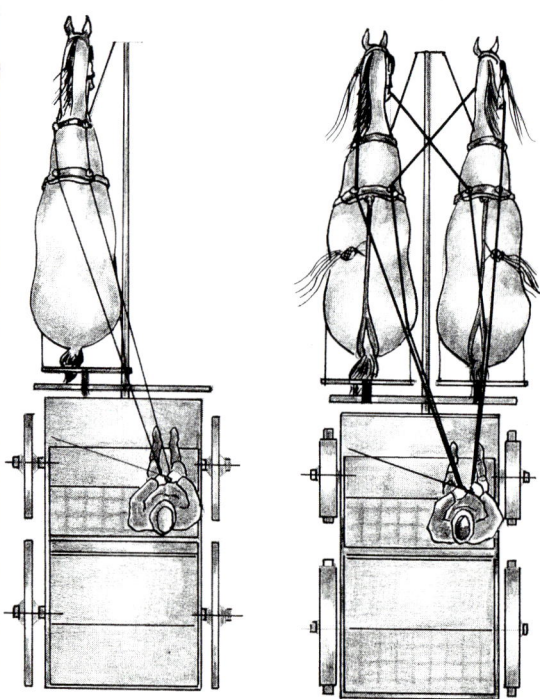

The position of the reins on teams drawing style carriages
One-horse vehicle (dog-cart)
Carriage-and-pair—carts and carriages for driving have the swingle-trees mounted onto the double-tree

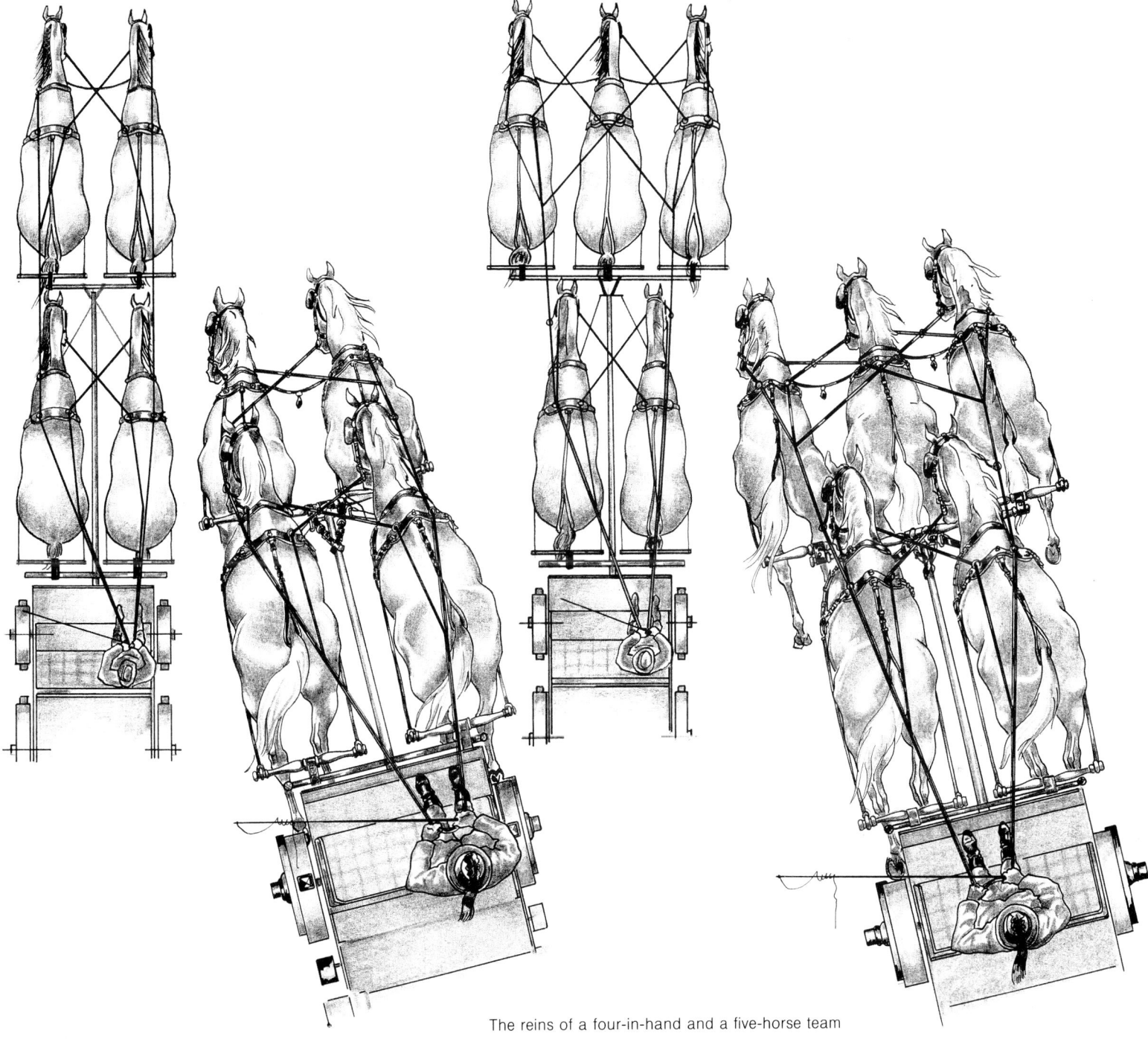

The reins of a four-in-hand and a five-horse team

Breeds for Coaching and for Driving Events

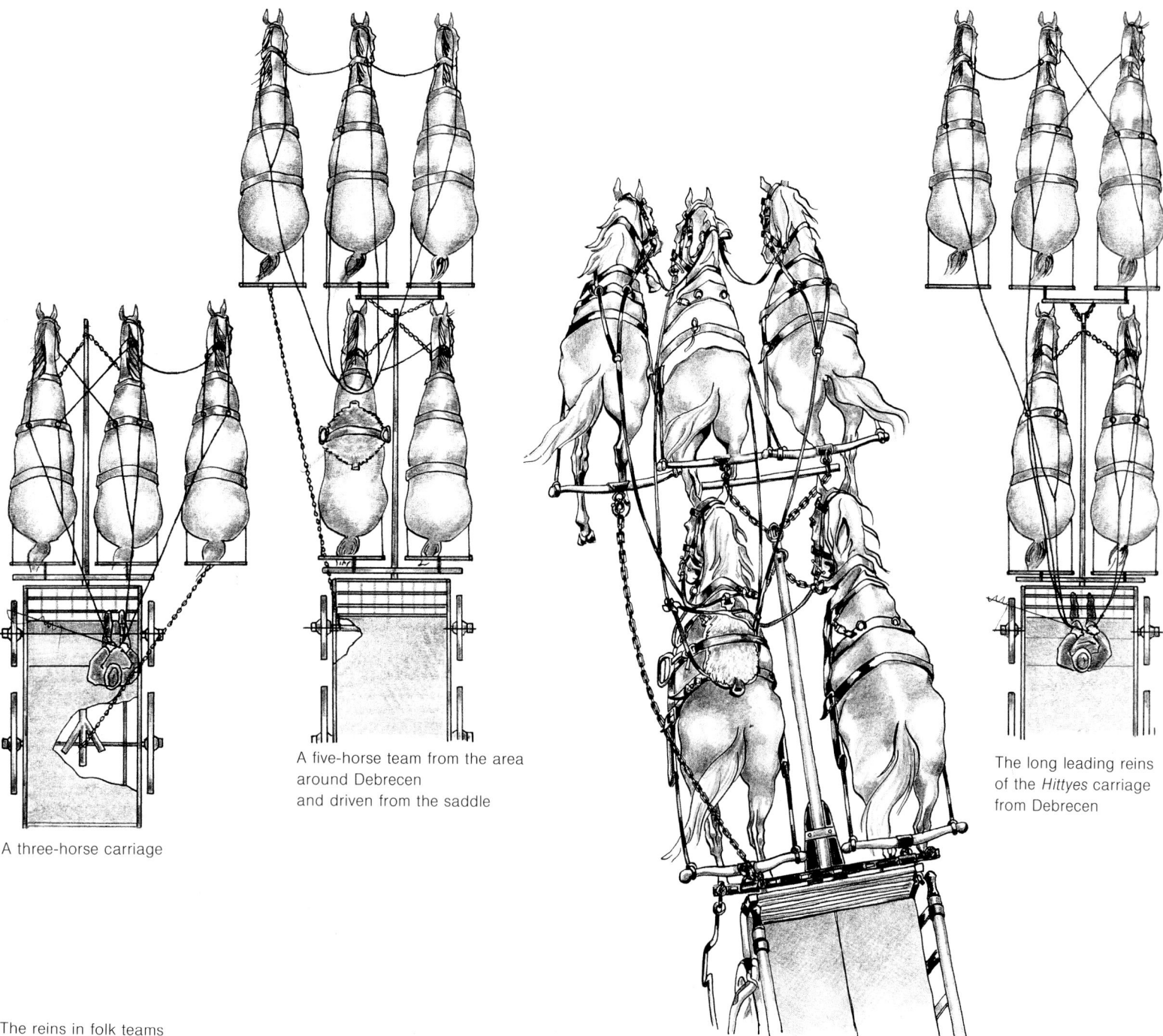

A five-horse team from the area around Debrecen and driven from the saddle

The long leading reins of the *Hittyes* carriage from Debrecen

A three-horse carriage

The reins in folk teams

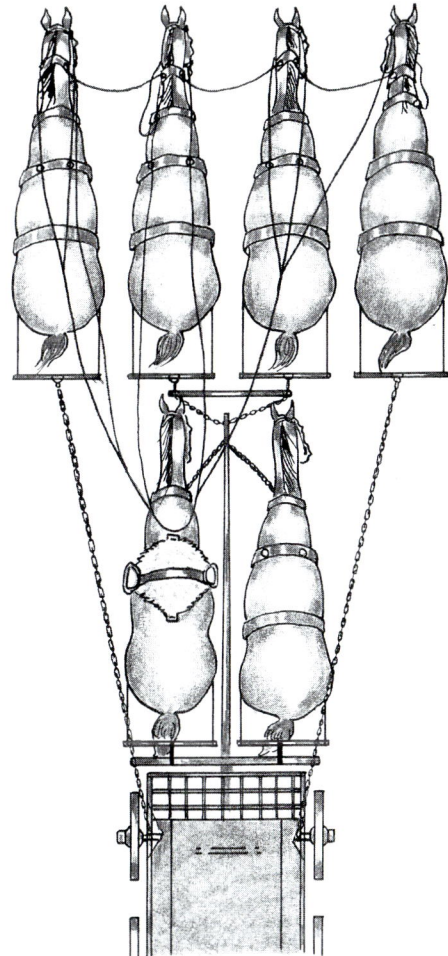

The reins in folk teams
A six-horse carriage from the Hajdúság driven from the saddle—the sixth horse is harnessed next to the right leader and both side horses are linked to the axle by a chain

immediately a four-in-hand; within one breed fundamental differences in appearance and temperament are likely to be much less than those arising when attempting to make up a team from different breeds. This solution is of course more demanding for a higher number of horses have to be tested, and what is more, a good deal of practice and skill is required.

In putting together a team, studs of a single

12 Hungarian six-horse carriage. Driver: Viktor Mátyus. Lipizaner stock brood mares from the State Farm of Szilvásvárad

breed are always given preference and this uniformity guarantees a significant advantage in the choice of horses. The favourable appearance in a pure-bred stud can only be profitable, if it has a sufficient number of horses. A four-in-hand team can only be kept with certainty for a number of years, if the stud has at its disposal a stock of thirty to forty brood mares.

Carriage-driving as a sport in Hungary is concentrated mainly on government owned stock-breeding farms and on agricultural co-operatives. At present there are seventeen state-owned farms and thirty co-operatives engaged in stock-breeding (two of which are significant). Each stud has at least thirty stock brood mares, the majority have even more. The activities of these farms are complemented by horse breeding on an individual scale, where the characteristics of the landscape and its traditions are reflected in so-called local area-breeds, however, they are less and less conspicuous due to changes in population. Therefore, there are enough possibilities for the replacement of horses for competitive teams. Several places have recently made attempts to breed special "team horses". Results of systematic cross-breeding show that these efforts are in the right direction. Offspring resulting from the crossing of a Lipizaner trotter and a Hungarian half-bred trotter have proved to be very successful coach-horses.

The Arab

The blood of the Arab horse can be found in a greater or smaller proportion in every breed. Even today, Arabs are widely used as regenerators to correct defects or to preserve good qualities.

During the thousand years of breeding activities the breed has become genetically stable, it inherits well its characteristic features and qualities. The main breeding farm in Hungary is Bábolna. The Bábolna Arab is stockier and more muscular than a pure-bred, therefore it is suitable for coaching as well. In making the choice out of one blood line, a very representative team can be formed.

At Bábolna carriage-driving has become a real cult. The stud has generated real coaching dynasties and they have presented the art of Hungarian driving till today.

Tibor Pettkó-Szandtner, author of **Magyar kocsizás** ("Coaching in Hungary"), 1931, lived and worked, in charge of the stud, at Bábolna. His book was the first summarized work on this subject.

Coaches drawn by Arab horses are, however, inadequate to comply with the demands of contemporary competitive events. The particular physique of the Arab horse is considered to be the prime reason why it is unable to keep within the walking time allowed for marathon events.

On the other hand, so-called Anglo-Arab

13 Anglo–Arab carriage-and-pair. Driver: István Fehér, Dombóvár

A seven-horse team from Debrecen, driven from the saddle
1. saddled horse 2. off-wheeler 3. rein horse
4. off-leader (trace horse) 5. left chain horse
6. right chain horse 7. right side (relay) horse

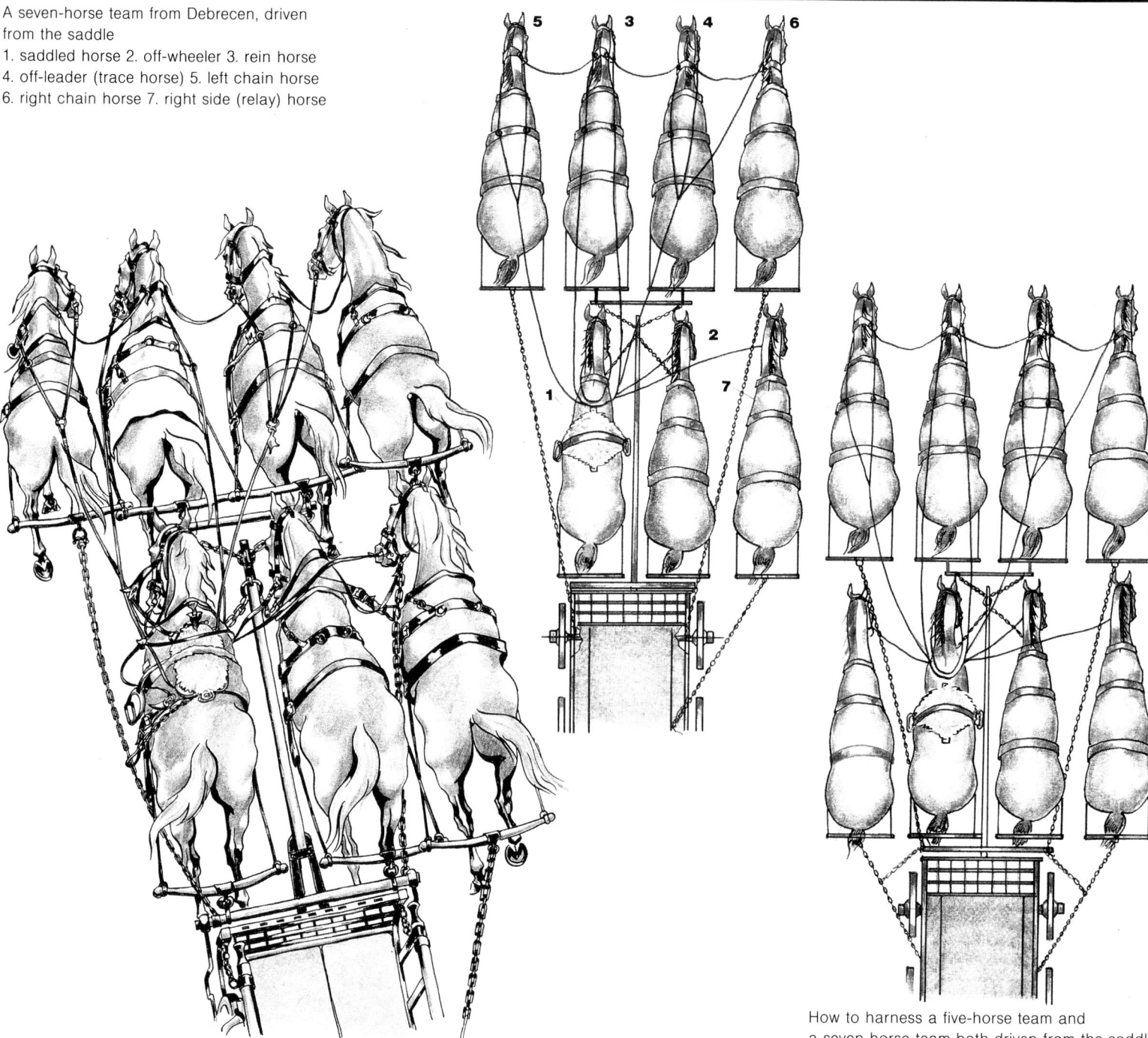

How to harness a five-horse team and a seven-horse team both driven from the saddle

horses resulting from the crossing of the Arab with the English thoroughbred have properly held their ground in the extremely testing conditions of both European and World Championships. Hungary has also chosen an Anglo-Arab carriage-and-pair (driver Mrs Fehér) to be sent to the world competitions. Anglo-Arab four-in-hands from Poland have been regular participants at international events. Therefore, in breeding coachhorses the Anglo-Arab deserves special attention. For instance, foals born in Hungary from a Shagya Arab stallion and an English blood mare have proved to be perfect carriage horses. Stocky, even-tempered English blood mares which are not sufficiently fast on race courses are sired by Arab stallions in order to obtain suitable harness horses.

The Lipizaner

Carriage-driving in Hungary owes a great deal to the Lipizaner breed, a fact testified to by the international successes of László Kádár, Imre Abonyi and György Bárdos. All three have achieved excellent results with Lipizaner four-in-hands.

The most important Lipizaner stud in Hungary is at Szilvásvárad, where eighty mares ensure the continuation of this race. The Kinizsi Agricultural Co-operative of Bana with twenty mares is also a Lipizaner stud. To sum up, Hungary is well populated with Lipizaner horses. Drivers can choose their horses whose blood line is determined by one sire and, furthermore, the female line may also be traced back so that a racing team can consist of related horses. As the Lipizaner has always displayed excellent birthrate, there are sufficient numbers of young foals for selection.

A Lipizaner begins to move properly only after three or four hours of schooling, while other breeds need only one and a half to two hours. The fact that the Lipizaners oblige drivers to train them longer and more often, also improves the driver's skill. In this sense the Lipizaner "educates" the driver and this is a further advantage of the breed. Only those who have enough time, patience and diligence should harness a Lipizaner. While training a team, drivers must be ready to sacrifice a good deal of their spare time and to dedicate themselves to this noble sport, if they are to have any hope of success.

At the Lipizaner stud at Fogaras, horses are prepared for an aptitude test in drawing a carriage and selection follows accordingly. This activity started about a hundred years ago and increased dramatically after the Second World War. In a country lying in ruins the Lipizaner, working as a draught horse on the land played an important part in the return to normal life. The Szilvásvárad Stud had, first of all, the task of breeding coach and plough horses and only since 1972 have animals been selected especially for harness racing. Lipizaner studs take stallions and breeding mares only after they have passed a harness test.

In the selection of potential stock-breeding mares the animals are required precise tasks in order to see whether they will be suitable for competitive carriage-driving.

Requirements for stallions are more strict, and only those which have performed well at international competitions in the carriages of László Kádár and György Bárdos are used for breeding purposes. These facts make it obvious why it is mainly the Lipizaner which is favoured for driving in Hungary.

The Lipizaner has always been handicapped by exceeding the time allowed in the walking sections of the marathon and even today this is an unsolved problem. However, the walking time can be improved by sufficient practice. A good and time-honoured method is to make the horse repeatedly walk down a slope. Regular work in a yoke also improves the walking and this is even recommended in the autumn and winter off-seasons. Much patience and ambitious training are necessary to teach the Lipizaner to walk in the way that accords to time regulations in competition.

In Hungary, the actual stocks make it possible to put together and to maintain about four teams. This quantity may seem to be rather limited, but for many years qualified drivers have been able to succeed with them and so there is a great hope for the future of continuing this tradition.

The Nonius

The Nonius was bred primarily to meet the requirements of the Hungarian Army for light artillery and draught horses; at the same time the Nonius was a valuable asset in agriculture. Even nowadays, the Nonius is important in farming in the Great Hungarian Plain.

The stock of warm-blooded Nonius breeding mares is estimated to be about 3,000 animals. The pure-bred Nonius is raised in the State Stud of Mezőhegyes and Hortobágy, as well as in other agricultural co-operatives. There are also many in private and other stocks.

14 The competition four-in-hand of the State Farm of Szilvásvárad drawn by Lipizaner stock brood mares. Driver: Viktor Mátyus

Breeds for Coaching and for Driving Events

The Nonius is the second largest breed (after the Hungarian Half-Bred) suitable for carriage-driving and is therefore of great importance for all who are involved in this sport. Many fine teams owe their success to this breed. The stud of the Agricultural Complex at Mezőhegyes cherishes the tradition of breeding and preparing four-in-hands of black Nonius stallions for competitive events. The Hortobágy State Farm has a record of success with teams of Nonius chestnut mares.

As in other recognized breeds, uniformity of appearance is one of the most appreciated characteristics of the Nonius. It breeds true to colour: either chestnut or black. Black horses are often rashly proclaimed to be Hungarian half-breds, but thorough investigation often reveals Nonius blood.

Experts have recently attempted to cross Nonius with other breeds. The most notable crossings have been with English thoroughbreds, trotters and other German lines (i.e. Aldato, especially bred for competitions).

The Nonius is somewhat stocky, uniform in appearance, and is not only willing but capable of strenuous work. It is, however, an easy mover and in temperament and movement is not immediately suitable for jumping or carriage-driving.

The crossing of the Nonius with trotters has been attended by success. Gábor Fintha, who has repeatedly been selected to represent Hungary in driving events has a competitive team of this type.

Considering the relatively big population, pure-blood breeding of the Nonius presents no problems; only as many mares should be crossed as prospective demand for offspring requires. The animals resulting from crossings are not used for further breeding.

To sum up, a Nonius four-in-hand is certainly good enough to reach the required expectations, but considerable patience is required in finding the right animals. On the other hand, a Nonius crossed with a trotter gives a first-class carriage-horse, and already a single crossing ensures a series of reliable animals.

15 Competition four-in-hand drawn by cream-coloured Hungarian Half-Bred horses

16 Five-horse carriage of the town of Debrecen, drawn by Nonius stallions

The Hungarian Half-Bred

This breed is the most numerous in Hungary and promises the best prospects for selection. The traditional Half-Breds of Kisbér and Mezőhegyes (Furioso and North Star) still exist as well as the Gidran, and besides the warm-blooded breed they are represented to different degrees in the blood line of the country's other stocks.

A new era has just begun for the Hungarian Half-Bred. The fact that horses were no longer needed in the army or in agriculture, and that their principal future lay in sport was recognized at the beginning of the 1950s. Qualified studs began the selection and import of animals from those countries (mainly from West Germany), whose horses had performed outstandingly at major world competitions and Olympic Games.

Obviously refinement in breeding is still in its infancy: the change from generation to generation is quite slow, and only prolonged persistent effort can lead to concrete results. The past ten years have been a period of trial and error. Though, it must be admitted that genuine progress has been registered from which competitive-harness sport has also profited.

The development of horses of suitable frame, stature and movement, combined with the practice of open grazing guarantee excellent and ever-improving quality, so that the actual stock of the Hungarian Half-Bred is an encouraging basis for the future of harness events of all kinds.

Sándor Fülöp and Ferenc Muity through their outstanding international results with Hungarian Half-Bred teams have demonstrated the aptitude of this type for coaching. However, the driver who intends to put together a four-in-hand of Hungarian Half-Breds does not have an easy task. Compared to the previously mentioned breeds, the Hungarian Half-Bred is more heterogeneous.

How, then, should a successful team be put together?

Uniformity of appearance is important. Moreover, the blood line should be checked by all means. If possible, the progeny of one sire

17 Competition four-in-hand drawn by the offspring resulting from the crossing of the Nonius and the Trotter. Driver: Gábor Fintha, Hortobágy State Farm

18 Competition four-in-hand of the Agricultural Complex of Mezőhegyes, drawn by Nonius—Holstein F_1 horses. Driver: Sándor Krizsán

19 The team of the Hungarian People's Republic driving in the marathon at a championship event. Driver: Sándor Fülöp. The team is made up of horses bred from the crossing of the Orlov Trotter and the Lipizaner

should be chosen. If the maternal line can be traced back as well, then a real family of blood-related horses can be harnessed.

First of all pairs should be selected and then four-in-hand teams should be formed out of these pairs. The ideal is to be in position to select from eight to ten pairs. It is advisable to put reliable, even-tempered large framed horses near to the swingle-tree, while lively, easy-turning ones should come to the front. It does not matter if these animals in front are less stocky than the others, but there should be no marked difference between leaders and wheelers. Therefore, carriage-horses should always be bought in pairs and never singly. (They can be tested in the stud.)

All this is important in order to avoid some of the most common mistakes. If horses are selected singly, problems are always likely to arise. It may be extremely difficult to find the suitable fourth animal, or one of the wheelers may not fit into the team.

The Trotter and its Cross-Breeds

Hungarian drivers have a lot to do with Trotters and the offspring resulting from crossing. Hungarian drivers and specialists are of the opinion that, in future, not the pure-blood breeds but their Trotter-crossed varieties (hybrids) will probably prove to be the most favoured types in carriage-driving.

Results obtained so far clearly demonstrate the efficiency of carriages using crossed breeds such as Trotter+Lipizaner, Trotter+Hungarian Half-Bred and Trotter+Nonius.

Normally, the pure-bred Trotter is rather small in stature, tends to have leg defects and unattractive gait. Crossing has largely eliminated these disadvantages; the Half-Bred possesses all the necessary qualities for carriage-driving, such as an attractive appearance, good work-capatiy, generous movements and competitive spirit. Breeders of the traditional types are recommended to have mares of working disposition covered by Trotter stallions from time to time.

Occasional, deliberate cross-breeding does not jeopardize the preservation of a stock and facilitates production of harness horses. The progeny of cross-bred horses should be considered end-products; further breeding is not recommended.

In Hungary, the Hungarian—Soviet Friendship Agricultural Co-operative at Kecskemét is concerned with cross-breeding to produce special harness horses under the guidance of Sándor Fülöp, a world champion. Here, Lipizaner mares are crossed with Orlov Trotter stallions, selected long ago by Imre Abonyi. We speak in this case of a rotative crossing aiming at the stabilization of a fifty per cent ratio of Lipizaner and Trotter blood. The first generation (F1) holds out promise. It is to be hoped that this successful pioneer work will continue and the animals bred in this way will provide good raw material for driving.

Hungarian Carriages and the Marathon Vehicle

Linguistics shows that the origin of the word "coach" and its equivalent in many European languages is the Hungarian word *kocsi*. It is derived from the Hungarian **kocsi, szekér** or wagon of Kocs. The village of Kocs in Hungary is considered to be the home of the coach-builders who built the first light and fast carriages. These are facts that testify to Hungary's long tradition in professional coach-building.

According to their usage, present day competition vehicles are divided into two groups: road carriages and cross-country carriages. (Carts and state coaches will only be briefly mentioned as they are not used for competitions.) The style carriages have preserved tradition, while cross-country vehicles are built for competition.

Due to a certain regression in the artisan-based coach-building industry, contemporary carriages are rather expensive. The high costs and the modification of the competition rules combine to favour a preference for the cross-country type of carriages in competitive events rather than exposing the expensive style carriages, which are so hard to obtain, to the danger of possible damage.

Style is not stipulated, only weight in the regulations concerning the construction of cross-country carriages and so the best use can be made of modern technology.

Style Carriages Used for Dressage and Presentation

The Hungarian drivers' favourite carriage is the "Esterházy" or "Cseklész". This vehicle is designed angularly, has no side-opening, its mudguards are straight and the hood, too, is angular. Ornamentation is made of imitation cane-weave carved into the side-boards. The simple form, proper distribution of weight, manœuvrability and the traditional building methods are the basic essentials of its popularity.

An improved variety is the "Cziráky". The decoration of this carriage is the same: imitation carved cane-work, but its openings are

Hungarian coaching liveries
"Körösi" carriage, iron fittings

Hungarian Carriages and the Marathon Vehicle

The chassis of a wagon

1. Axle
2. Axle-centre
3. Axle-pin
4. Axle-head
5. Linchpin
6. Axle-flange
7. Axle-casing
8. Wheel hub bush
9. Axle-head strip
10. Rear board-joist
11. Perch
12. Grip of perch
13. Ironwork on the perch
14. Perch-ring
15. Strip
16. Perch-wing ironwork
17. Perch rubber
18. Idle nail
19. Perch nail
20. Perch-wing rod
21. Clasping strip
22. Stanchion
23. Middle bolt
24. Float
25. Stud-stave
26. Front board-joist
27. Stanchion
28. Clasping strip
29. Shaft-wing
30. Shaft-wing ironwork
31. Shaft-wing track rod
32. Shaft-wing link
33. Bottom pole-carrier
34. Swingle-tree
35. Ironwork fixing the swingle-tree
36. Ironwork on the swingle-tree
37. End-ring on the swingle-tree
38. Rosette
39. Rod grummet
40. Track rod for the swingle-tree
41. Bottom trestle for the forage rack
42. Coupling unit
43. Double-tree (pair of scales)
44. Case for the double-tree
45. Stirrup piece for holding the double-tree
46. Harness support
47. Ring for holding the double-tree
48. Perch branch
49. Screw
50. Wheel bolt

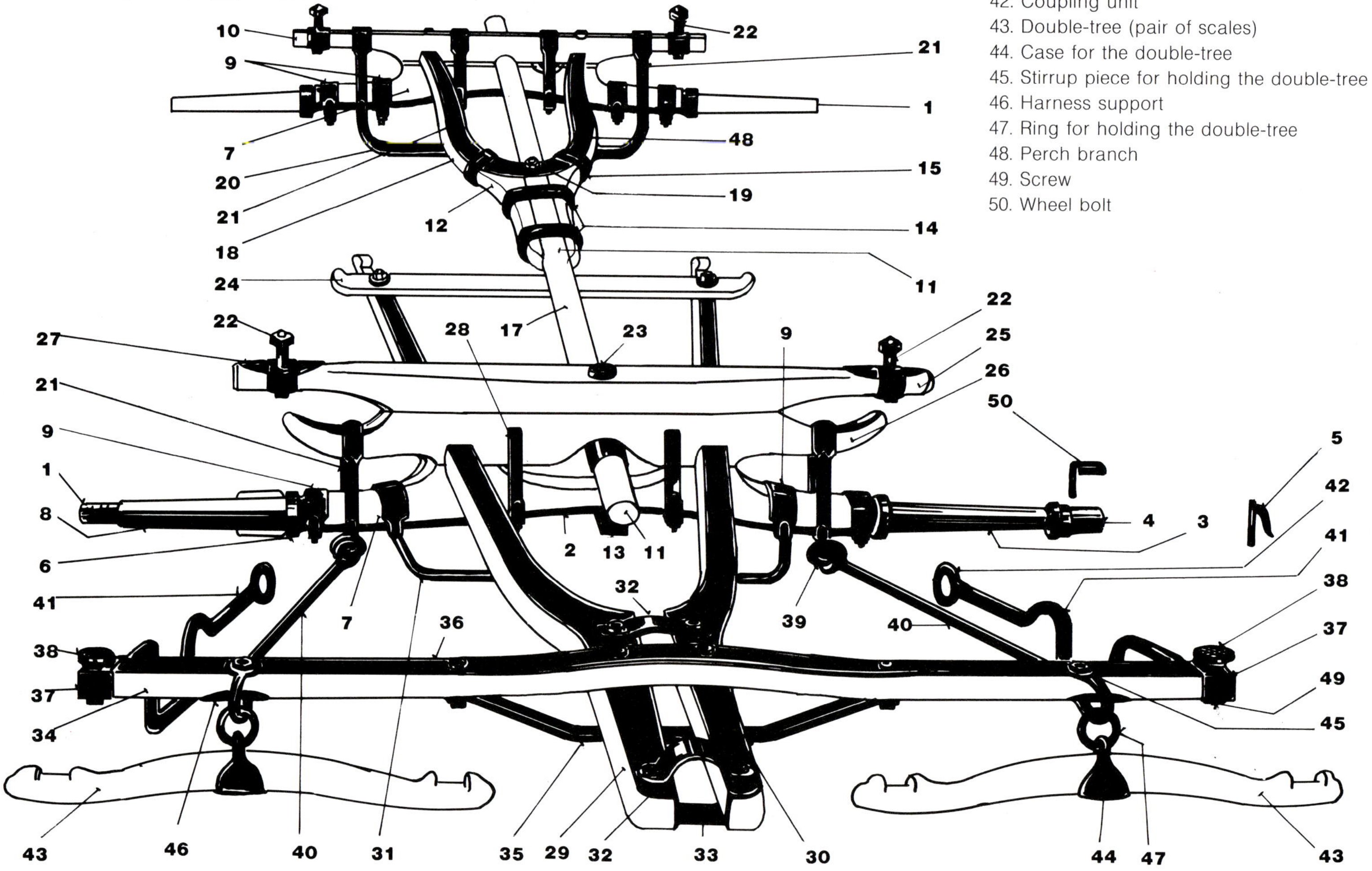

20 Rustic carriage of Jászság in 1969

Style Carriages for Dressage and Presentation

The chassis of a carriage for driving

1. Stud-stave
2. Ironwork supporting the fifth wheel
3. L-shaped component
4. Front view of the stud-stave
5. Fifth wheel
6. Greasy tread
7. Supporting iron for the fifth wheel
8. Greasy tread
9. Pinchbar
10. Middle bolt casing
11. Swingle-tree
12. Rod support
13. Main spring leaf
14. Rod support (front view)
15. "Moustache"
16. Grummet holding the double-tree
17. Round-wing
18. Fork pad
19. Double-tree centre
20. Double-tree nail
21. Screw for tightening the double-tree nail
22. Trace "nest"
23. End-part of the double-tree
24. Ring on the swingle-tree
25. Rosette on the swingle-tree
26. Round wing screw
27. Spring screw
28. Rod base

21 The "Károlyi" carriage or carriage of "Fót". The rear wheels have hydraulic foot-brakes

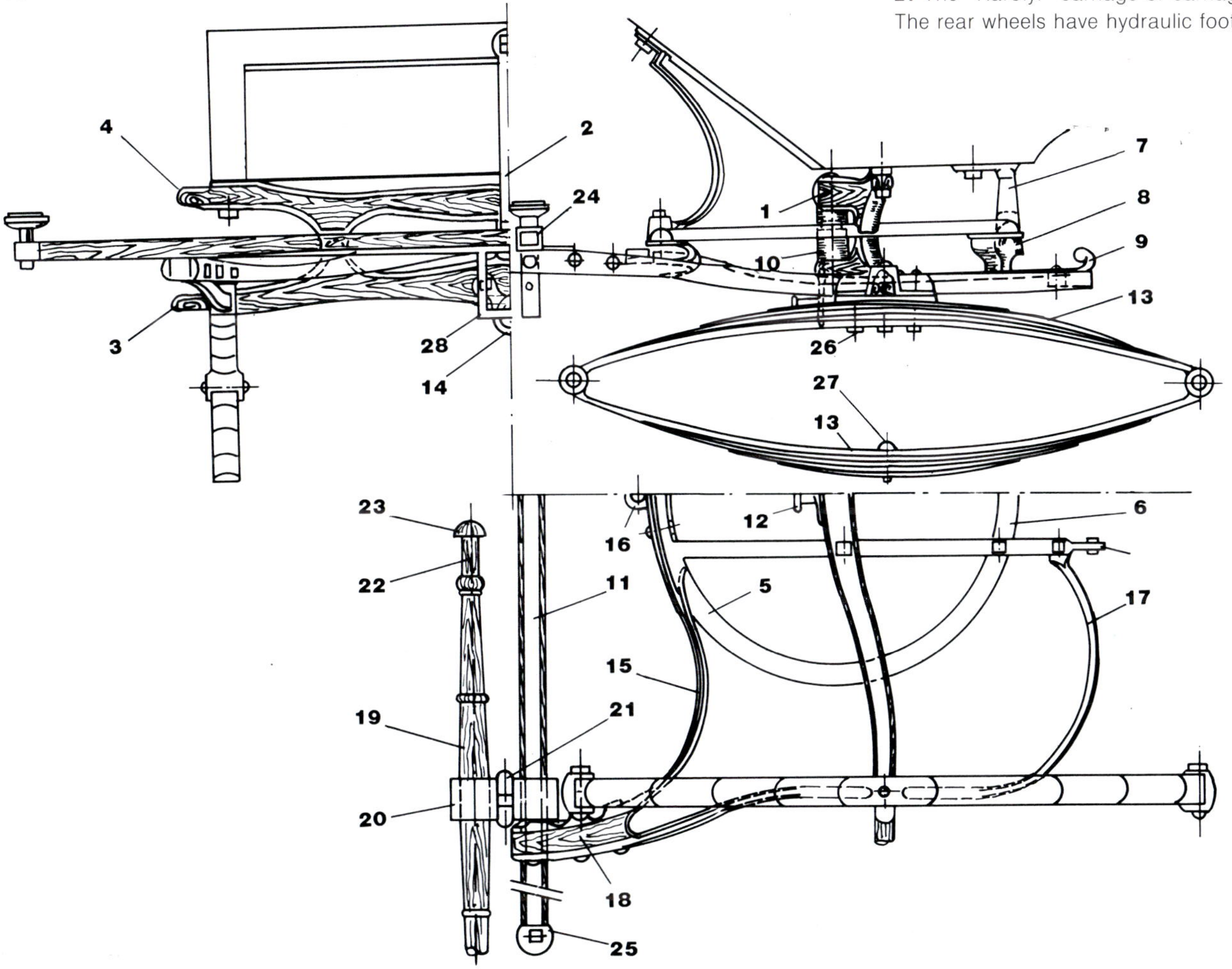

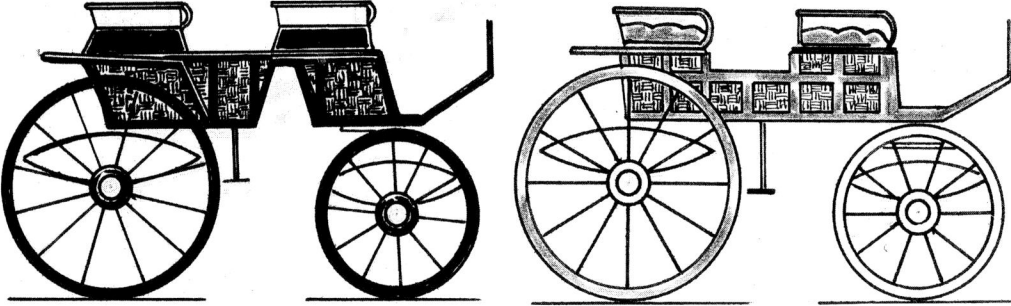

"Cseklész Esterházy" carriage   "Mór" carriage

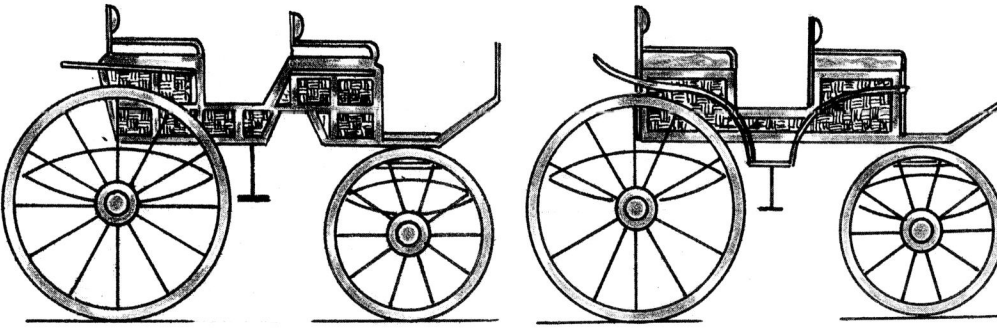

Hungarian carriage   "Károlyi" or "Fót" carriage

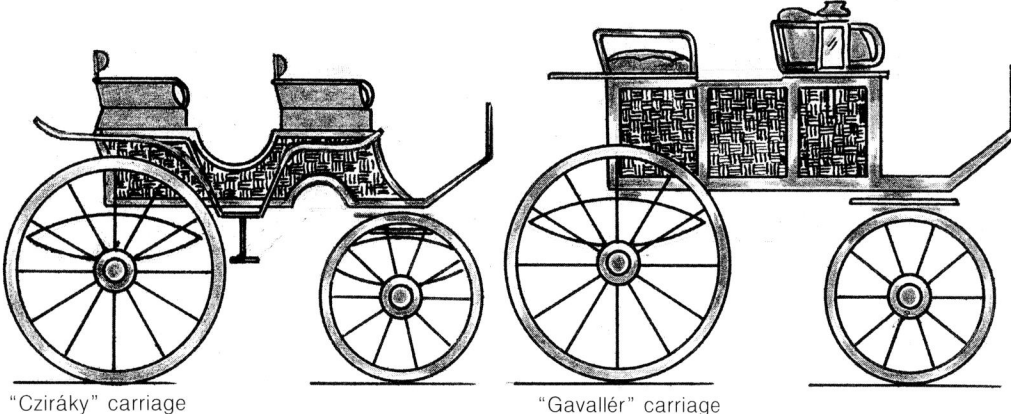

"Cziráky" carriage   "Gavallér" carriage

arched and the mudguards are also curved. All this gives the "Cziráky" a noble and gracious aspect. It has backed chairs inside.

The next most popular style carriage is the "Károlyi kocsi" or the carriage of "Fót". The side-boards have angular openings as well as the usual carved ornamentations in the form of cane-weave. The small, easy-turning wheels are a guarantee of good manœuvrability. The mudguards are curved.

These basic types of carriages have several derivations which are not necessarily in contrast to the original style, and are often more practical.

The so-called **gavallér kocsi** (cavalier carriage) is very light, made for privileged society, therefore the seat-box is designed very carefully. The groom and the assistant driver have to take the back seats.

The vehicle is very simple, shaped like a box and decorated by the usual carvings. The footboard to get to the back seats is mounted in the rear. Some of the more curved, new varieties are well-known as well; they fulfil the same tasks as those previously described. This is actually a carriage specially designed for competitive events. Being light, simple, easy to manœuvre, it is perfectly suited for a carriage-and-pair.

Vehicles known as "spider carts" or "buggies" are similar in design to the others, although they cannot be included in any of the above categories. There is no reason for depreciating these vehicles whose appearance is fully in keeping with Hungarian tradition, but to present them at significant events would probably represent a lack of style.

To be comprehensive, Hungarian wagons should be mentioned as well, as these are the prototype of all other coaches and carriages. In Debrecen and its environments the **bűrös szekér** (leather wagon) was employed for public transport up until the very last decades. Covered by a leather tent, this cart could serve well the passenger traffic between the town and the surrounding farms. It was simple, stable and reliable, even under miserable road conditions. All other carriages, even ceremonial coaches reflecting money, rank and power (like the Cor-

"Károlyi" carriage

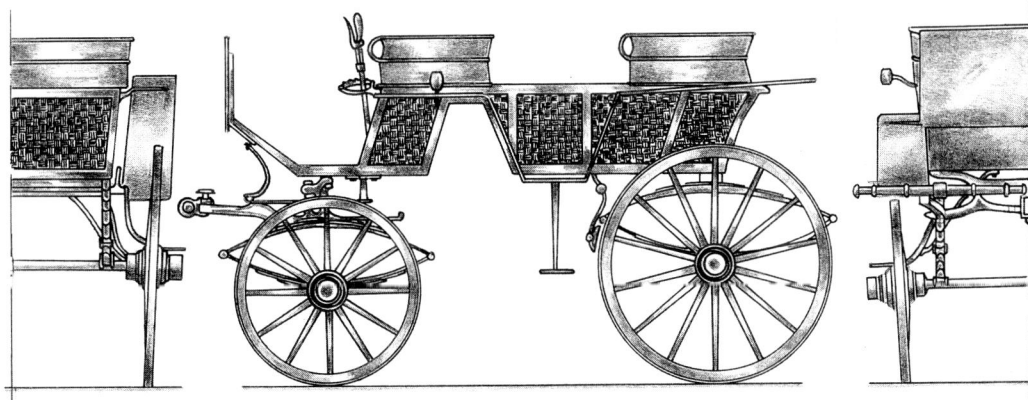

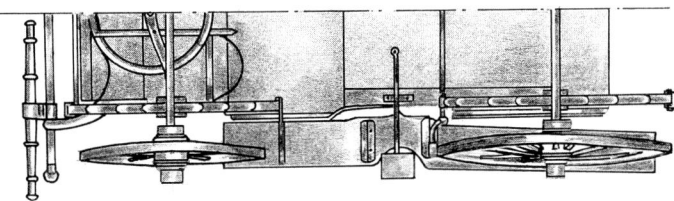

"Cseklész Esterházy" carriage

onation Coach) have been developed out of this very simple **bűrös kocsi.** This primaeval cart, probably originating from the time of the settlement of Magyar tribes in Hungary (ninth to tenth centuries A. D.), has survived in historical movies. For a few years travelling slaughterers used similar carts covered by canvas instead of leather.

The history of Hungarian coach-building and some of its masterpieces are exhibited in the Coach Museum of Parád. A visit to this museum is warmly recommended to all those who desire to extend their knowledge of coaches.

Cross-Country Carriages Used for the Marathon

This is the second large important group of modern carriages, and so we shall try to present them in more detail.

It would be rather difficult to describe the exact design of these carriages. They vary a great deal but the basic aim of the design is practicality and utility.

Some drivers insist on maintaining the original style while the fittings are of iron or some other inexpensive metal so as to avoid serious damage and loss in case the carriage should overturn, run against a tree or get stuck. The other extreme is when the shape of the coachbox as a whole looks rather like a lunar vehicle and merely the four wheels and the horses indicate that it is a carriage.

Drawing on general and technical experience and relying on the practice of leading Hungarian drivers, we shall enumerate all the main parameters of the ideal cross-country carriage.

Practicability embraces three important factors:
— resistance
— stability
— manœuvrability

At the same time, the fully equipped carriage must have a gross weight of at least 600 kg, excluding the driver and his assistants. Even the slightest excess would be unreasonable, whereas event-rules do not allow even 1 kg less.

Stability based on the correct distribution of

weight is the most important requirement. It means that the centre of gravity has to be located at the level of the axles, i.e. on the middle line between the two seats.

Calculations submitted by the coach-building industry show that the following distribution of weight is the most efficient:

weight of the axles 110 kg/piece	total	220 kg
wheels .... 25 kg/piece	total	100 kg
springs .... 25 kg/piece	total	100 kg
fifth wheel-system together with the whipple trees	total	65 kg
pole + swingle-trees	total	25 kg
coach-box	total	70 kg
spare equipment	total	20 kg
total weight of the carriage ...	total	600 kg

The above specifications, however, can be improved. The distribution of weight, as well as a transfer of the centre of gravity (to the front or to the back), can usually be influenced by the axles' weight. For instance, if the front axle is lighter and the rear one heavier, the centre of gravity shifts backwards and manœuvrability improves.

We shall enumerate, as follows, the most essential parts of a cross-country carriage, paying special attention to their stability and manœuvrability.

Axles

Two important questions arise in connection with the axles:
1. width of the wheel-tracks
2. The type of bearing to be used at the end of the axles.

The ideal wheel-gauge is between 130 and 135 cm. With a narrower gauge, the vehicle is liable to overturn, especially if encountering natural obstacles or in taking sharp bends. With a wider gauge the carriage is less manœuvrable and more likely to get stuck.

With regard to the second question, slide-bearings are highly recommended, especially the well-oiled Colling. Some competition drivers have tried to use ball-bearings, but these are not resistant enough to lateral forces. In cross-country events, wheels and bearings are very often exposed to heavy lateral forces which

22 Cross-country carriage

23 Cross-country carriage

24 Hit-guards on the wheels of a cross-country carriage

25 Fixing of the pole-end and of the swingle-tree by ropes before the marathon starts

26 Cross-country carriage. The wheel guards are against hitting and sticking. All parts which might cause the vehicle to get stuck are rounded off

27 Cross-country carriage

28 Stair-step and mudguards are superfluous on cross-country carriages as they may cause difficulties by getting stuck

may result in the loosening of the wheels; in less serious cases, the ball-bearings may break obliging the driver to retire from the competition. The fitting of ball-bearings requires greater knowledge, skill and equipment than that of slide-bearings. Furthermore, not even the fastest carriage-wheels ever reach a speed of more than 100 rpm (revolutions per minute), which makes ball-bearings unnecessary.

Wheels

Traditionally wheels are made of wood. The rims should be made of steamed beech or ash; the spokes of acacia or ash and the hub of elm. Before it is ready for use timber for wheel-making should be stored for at least five years in an airy, dry warehouse, piled up professionally. Good wheels cannot be manufactured from plain wood, and it is as well to know that two to three-year-old timber is still considered to be plain.

In comparison with other materials, wooden wheels are more elastic and tough.

Some new cross-country carriages have a guard mounted between wheel-hub and rim to prevent jamming. This extra-security originates from international events in which Hungarian drivers learned from bitter experience. When negotiating an obstacle the end of the axle often got stuck and the spokes were either exposed to vigorous lateral pressure or even hit, so that the

29 The unique team of the Agricultural Co-operative of Máriapócs

wheel broke and the driver had to sit on the wheel-hub in order to complete the course. The rules of present-day international events specify that carriages must be in possession of all four wheels as they pass the finishing point. The exaggerated security measures are superfluous if the wheel-wright does a proper job by using adequately prepared timber and by mounting the hub in a way that the spokes do not interlock in the centre, but in the direction of the spoke-edges.

Cross-country carriages need very strong wheels, similar to those of dray-carts. The asymmetrical fastening of the spokes to the wheel-hub makes certain that the end of the hub does not project more than 5–7 cm. This reduces to a minimum the danger of becoming stuck.

It is worth placing strong iron tires on the wheels. Wheels made and maintained professionally are very resistant and safe.

Suspension

The springs used for cross-country carriages are generally either too hard or too soft. If suspension is very hard, it can damage or even break other parts of the carriage, while a too soft suspension reduces speed. Therefore, it is best to build in a shock-absorber, as in motorcars, and this should be done, in all cases, by a skilled worker.

Fifth Wheel

The shape of the fifth wheel is constant, but for cross-country carriages they must be made of stronger material. The quality of welding is very important, since a great number of defects are attributable to bad joints.

Carriages with a fifth wheel made of pure iron are much too stiff. Hard timber logs and other fittings increase smooth driving, and although this necessitates regular controls and servicing, the additional work is rewarding. The foot-board, which is a part of the fifth wheel, is made of wood (ash or acacia) as well; an iron fastening on the bottom increases stability. Experience shows that the most efficient material-composition for the fifth wheel is wood combined with iron.

Swingle-Trees

These are also made of wood; usually ash or acacia. Lathe-turned swingle-trees are not suitable; they break too easily. The design should be copied from the swingle-trees used for dray-carts. The double-tree should be fastened to the swingle-tree by straps. Chains, clips and screws have not proved suitable. They are either too stiff or too loose. The straps winding around the double-tree and the swingle-tree are fixed by special nuts. (An iron rectangle is welded on top of the screw-head and a similar washer is placed under the nut.) A tightly screwed-up nut keeps the straps properly together. After usage the straps should be cleaned and smeared with leathergrease. When cracks develop they should be replaced.

Pole

Poles are usually made of ash-wood. Birch is mainly used for style carriages, as they are less heavy. Care has to be taken to split the wood along the grain. A pole-break can result in serious accidents even over level courses.

Poles have been made recently coated with polyester (7–8 mm) and fortified by glass fibre. This is an excellent method. It gives enormously increased flexibility and the pole is virtually unbreakable. The polyester coating should cover the whole of its length, i.e. up to the case on the pole-end.

The length is also very essential. It should be adjusted to the size of the horse so that the pole-end and the horse's nose (when held naturally) should be aligned. A pole which is too

30 Cross-country carriage fixed by ropes and prepared for the marathon

Cross-Country Carriages

31 This swingle-tree is wrongly mounted, as it projects over the side line of the carriage and will cause it to stick

32 The pole and the swingle-trees are fixed by ropes before the marathon starts

33 The method of fitting the foot-brake and the main-brake cylinder

long hinders the carriage when mounting obstacles. The usual length of a pole is 270–300 cm. Other accessories are the so-called "spectacles" and the hook.

Coach-Box

The main requirement is again practicability. The "Cziráky" carriage provides the best example of a coach-box.

The best material for building a coach-box is steamed beech. The inside of the wooden frame should be coated with ironwork corresponding to the weight of the frame. Mudguards and foot-board are dispensed with. Not having any practical use, they would only increase the danger of getting stuck. The size and height of the seat-box are determined by the driver, he should feel comfortable, safe and able to support his feet properly on the foot-board. The newest type of carriages have two wide foot-boards in the rear, so the assistant drivers can easily keep the carriage under control and manoeuvre it through the obstacles.

Brakes

A good brake system increases manoeuvrability, as for instance a foot-operated brake leaves the driver's hands free. The rules make the hand-brake obligatory, the foot-brake is only optional, but strongly advisable. The best hydraulic foot-brake consists of two pedals close to each other, so that braking can be applied to the wheels on either side of the carriage or, by pressing both, simultaneous braking is possible as well. Most carriages in use today have a braking system for the rear wheels, but brakes stopping all four wheels simultaneously are seldom encountered.

It is much easier to manoeuvre the carriage in a sharp curve by using side-brakes. Nowadays, difficulties no longer arise in the mounting of such brakes (they are of advantage mainly in obstacle driving), and many drivers have them not only on cross-country carriages but even on the style ones.

Aesthetic aspects often do not justify the existence of hydraulic brakes on style carriages. However, there can be no objection to their mere existence, if they are mounted inconspicuously and do not affect the aesthetic value of the carriage. All this can be arranged these days and it should not be forgotten that carriages without hydraulic foot-brakes are definitely handicapped.

Other Fittings

The usual swingle-trees, upholstery, whip-socket, lamps, etc. might seem to be only minor accessories, but they are of considerable importance for the overall impression of a carriage, which can easily be spoiled by false fittings.

For the **ferrules of the pole-end** round forged breeching hooks and "spectacles" should be fitted. These ferrules are solid and so, even if the general finish is poor, the joints are not noticeable. Welded and cast ferrules are not reliable as they are rigid and break easily.

The **hooks of the swingle-tree** should be fitted on the pole's bottom as horses like to rub their heads, while resting, against the pole, and if the hook is on top of the pole, the bridle-buckle, the bit-ring or the rein might get caught in it.

Safety straps are another important part of swingle-trees. The two safety straps have to be pulled down on both sides of the iron ring in the middle of the swingle-tree which has to be hooked in and then, while clasping the pole, the straps have to be buckled in crosswise. In addition, this kind of strapping prevents whipple-trees from unnecessary swinging. Care must be taken not to buckle too tight and not to let the horses pull the carriage by the safety straps but only by the hook.

The safety straps on style carriages should have chased or simple brass buckles matching in style the strapping of the harness as a whole, while buckles on cross-country carriages should be made of steel plated with chromium or covered with rust-proof oil-paint.

An apparent trifle belonging to a carriage is the whip-socket. Style carriages usually have them made of turned wood, but leather or ant-

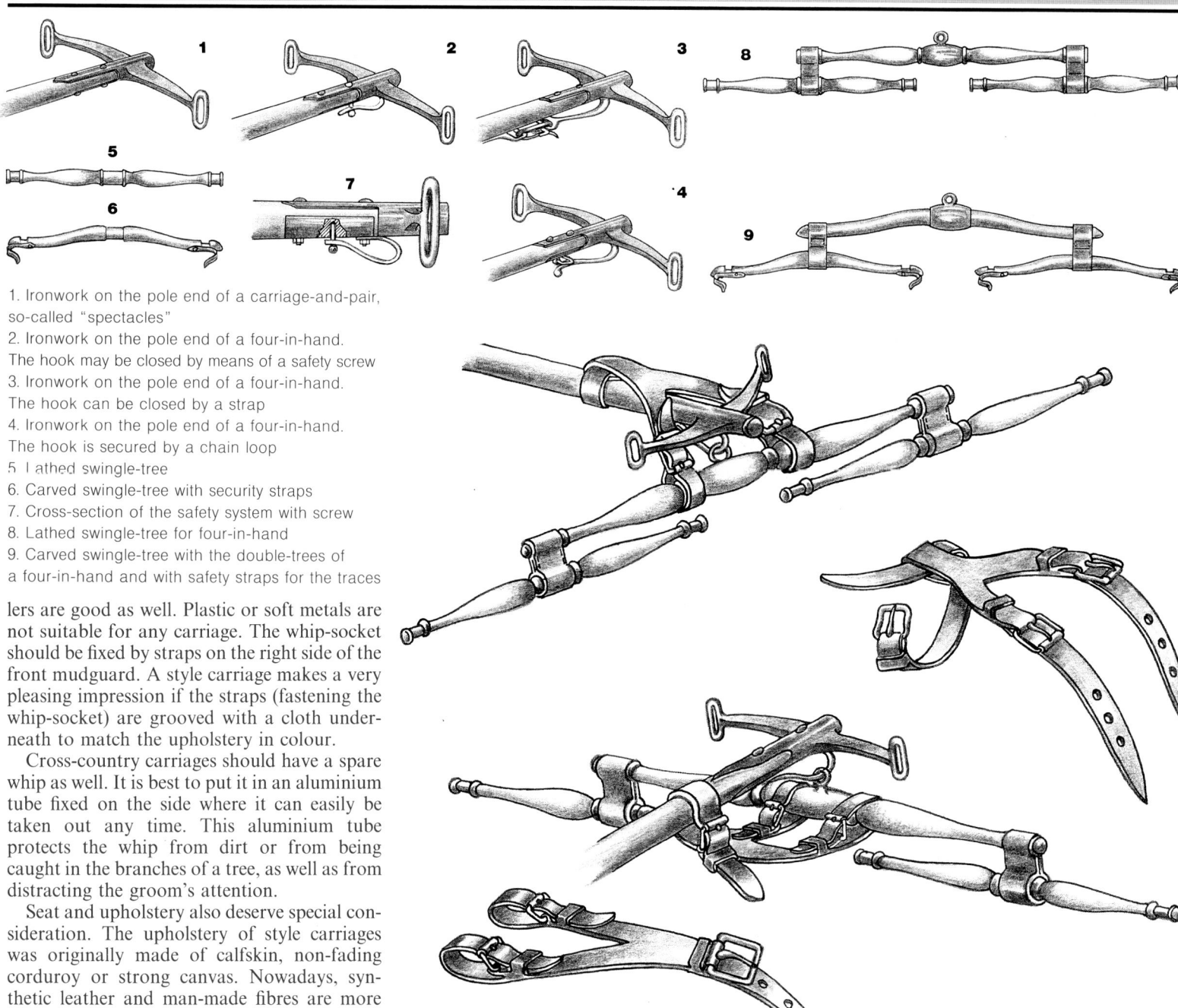

1. Ironwork on the pole end of a carriage-and-pair, so-called "spectacles"
2. Ironwork on the pole end of a four-in-hand. The hook may be closed by means of a safety screw
3. Ironwork on the pole end of a four-in-hand. The hook can be closed by a strap
4. Ironwork on the pole end of a four-in-hand. The hook is secured by a chain loop
5. Lathed swingle-tree
6. Carved swingle-tree with security straps
7. Cross-section of the safety system with screw
8. Lathed swingle-tree for four-in-hand
9. Carved swingle-tree with the double-trees of a four-in-hand and with safety straps for the traces

lers are good as well. Plastic or soft metals are not suitable for any carriage. The whip-socket should be fixed by straps on the right side of the front mudguard. A style carriage makes a very pleasing impression if the straps (fastening the whip-socket) are grooved with a cloth underneath to match the upholstery in colour.

Cross-country carriages should have a spare whip as well. It is best to put it in an aluminium tube fixed on the side where it can easily be taken out any time. This aluminium tube protects the whip from dirt or from being caught in the branches of a tree, as well as from distracting the groom's attention.

Seat and upholstery also deserve special consideration. The upholstery of style carriages was originally made of calfskin, non-fading corduroy or strong canvas. Nowadays, synthetic leather and man-made fibres are more common. Cloth made of natural fibre is more suitable for style carriages, whereas artificial leather is better for cross-country vehicles.

The belt-variety of safety strappings with "Y" straps

Cross-Country Carriages   27

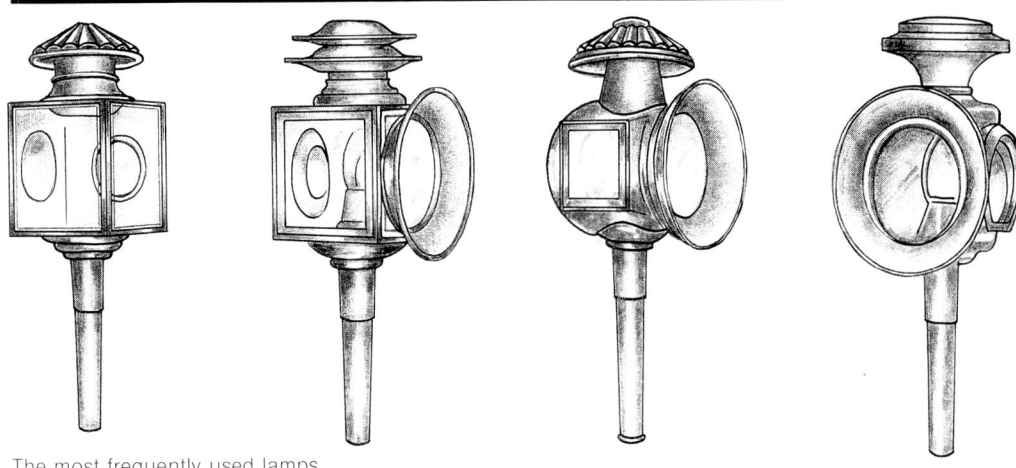

The most frequently used lamps

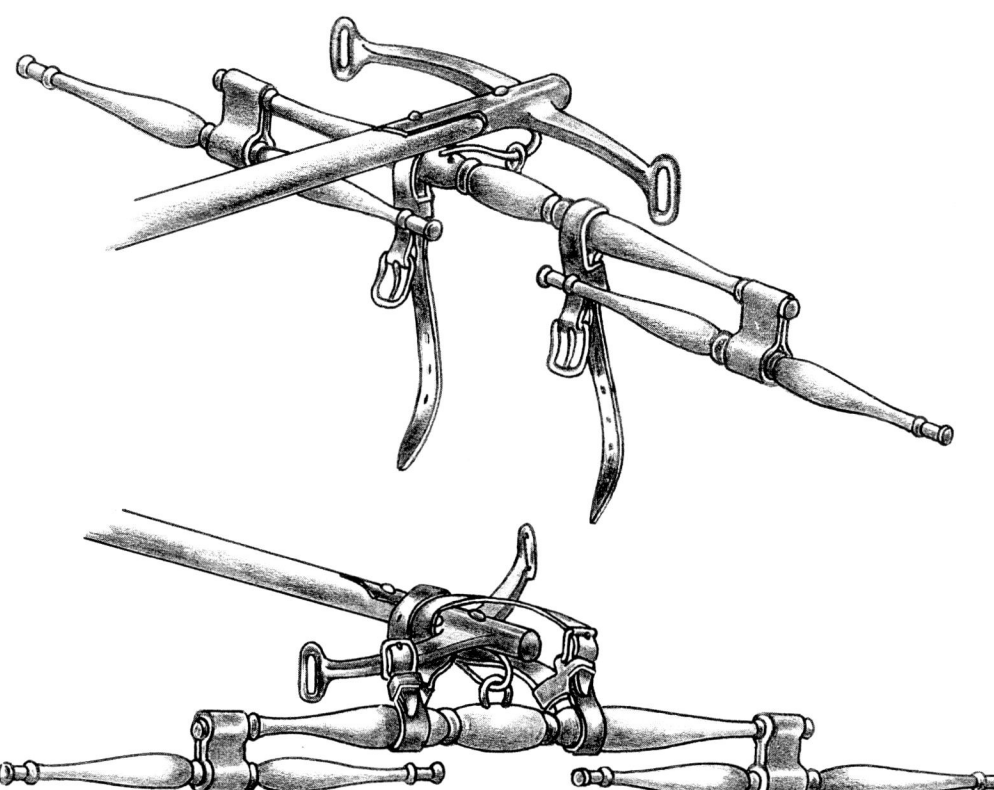

The mounting of the swingle-tree and buckling of the safety straps

The height of the seat should be about 45 cm above the carriage floor. The correct measurements are very important, as marathon events can last as much as one and a half hours, and one of the basic conditions to ensure a good performance is a safe seat.

The padded driver's seat ascends backwards, the thickness, the height and the incline are determined by the driver himself. The cartwright and the upholsterer work according to these specifications. The seats in cross-country carriages are doubly fixed, while those in style ones are not. The seat is mounted on the right side and is slidable in any direction. For instance, in obstacle driving some drivers prefer to sit in the middle of the carriage as they then have a better view on each side.

Lamps. In the course of time a great variety of different lamps have been invented. A decorative lamp finely wrought contributes largely to the appeal of the carriage.

Tradition requires lamps to be in harmony with the carriage as a whole. A carriage of curving lines needs rounded lamps, and an angular carriage (e.g. Esterházy) should have angular ones.

At the beginning, primitive carriages had candles inside the lamps. Technical progress first provided kerosene and gaslamps and, more recently, electric ones. As carriage-driving events never take place in the night, lamps are never judged by their capacity but by design, i.e. whether they fit the overall style of the carriage or not.

In agricultural co-operatives and on household farms carriages must have proper lighting, otherwise their use would not be allowed on public roads. The best solution is to put a lamp powered by a battery on the pole-end and two red rear lamps on the back of the carriage. An eventing carriage might have to be driven in the night, and therefore it is necessary to have in reserve a silver-plate battery rechargeable at any ordinary power-supply system, and a set of lamps which are easy to mount. There should be enough room in the coach-case for all these accessories.

Carriages should be kept in closed, covered sheds. Heating is unnecessary as it would only dry out the wood and the tenons and mortises are likely to come apart sooner.

After use, the carriage should be washed and dried with chamois leather. If necessary, some parts should be re-oiled. The painted inside surface is treated with a furniture polish, and if paint comes off somewhere, it should be restored at once, using the original colour. After the event is over, the wheels should be removed, and the leather parts, the suspension and the fifth wheel should be controlled.

Besides the event-vehicle, it is very useful to have training carriages as well. Lamps, straps, cushions and the pole should each have their own storage place, as e.g. a pole leant merely against the wall, will soon start to warp, which is undesirable.

At the end of the eventing season, a general overhaul should be made. Even the smallest parts of the carriage should be checked using every possible technical facility, such as X-rays to reveal whether there are extremely fine cracks in the ironwork. After the check-up all defective fittings should be replaced and, if necessary, the carriage should be repolished. If the vehicle is to stay in the shed for a longer period of time, it is advisable to balance the vehicle on a trestle, to take the weight off of the springs.

A properly maintained and well-prepared carriage not only spares the driver much annoyance but is more likely to bring success in later competitions.

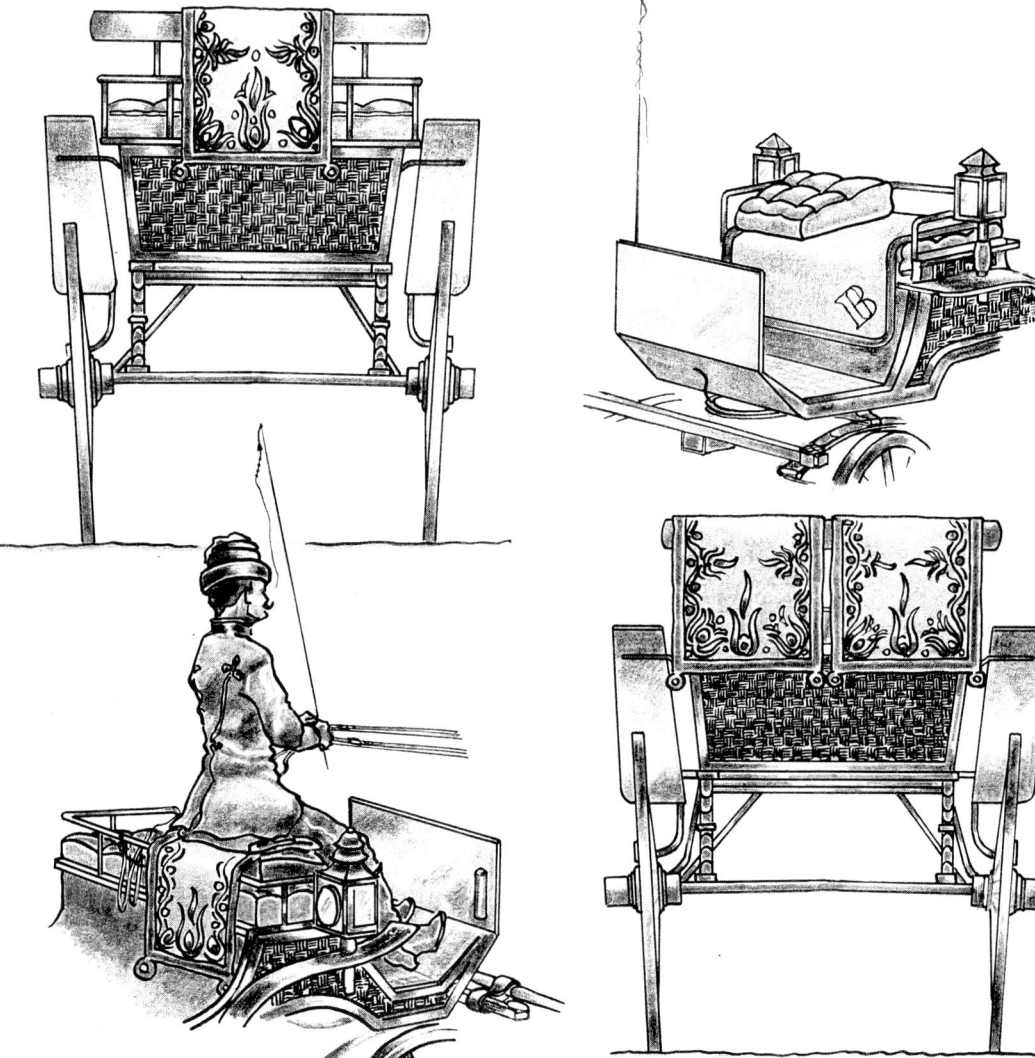

The correct way to drape the *szűr* and position the blankets. The correct position of the driver's seat

Hungarian Harnesses

The raw materials used for Hungarian harness are not as durable as the wood and metal used for carriages. This is the reason why only some buckles, strappings and metal decorations of ancient saddlery are still to be found. Leather relics are rather rare and their reconstruction is difficult.

The valuable collection of the Hungarian Agricultural Museum gives us an idea of the original style of harnesses, which can and should be preserved by all carriage-drivers, clubs and co-operatives. The world's two most acknowledged driving styles are the British and the Hungarian. The main differences between the two can be observed in harness, buckles, longe and bit. In Britain the collar-harness is popular while the breast-harness is preferred in Hungary.

The collar-harness does not tolerate any overdecoration (such as fringes) and each buckle and strap has its own special function.

In Hungary, carters used to employ a collar-harness lying close to the horse's body to make it easier for the horse to start hauling a heavy load. This harness, however, lacks the neck-strap and the breast-band which are quite natural for a Hungarian one.

The transfer of power takes place through the iron hames and the padding underneath over the traces. The back-strap together with the pommel, the girth and the crupper are to be found here exactly as in a Hungarian harness, although there is an additional belly-band as well.

The girth can have the bearing rein and other straps buckled to it, inside the terret which is at the bottom of the hame. Smaller straps are fastened to the hame, lying close on the horse's chest, run between the two fore-legs of the horse and are buckled to the belly-band (auxiliary girth). A Hungarian pair horse harness does not have a belly-band, while the front horses of a four-in-hand do to stop the traces from sliding upwards. The British driving style differs from that in Hungary in the longeing and buckling of the reins, as they are not connected by the "frog".

34 Kecskemét, 1978. Driving World Championship. Driver: Prince Philip of Edinburgh, member of the British team, former President of the FEI. The horses in Hungarian breast harness

In a British four-in-hand the driver has four reins in his hands or actually two pairs running from the leaders and wheelers. If going only for a pleasure-drive it would probably be no problem to handle all four reins separately. However, it is rather complicated and it may considerably hinder the driver's reactions at events. Participants in international competitions have

35 Wide, braided front decoration on a folk team from Hajdúszoboszló

give the impression of running back individually into the driver's hands without any buckles. Only the reins on one side are kept together by a loop and held together in the driver's hand (similarly to the four-in-hand) by the frog. In this way, all four reins are individually and precisely adjustable. The bits show the most striking differences.

The British collar-harness has a curb-bit with chain while the Hungarian driver prefers the four-ring driving bit. According to their sharpness and efficacy, Hungarian bits have a lot of different varieties corresponding to the sensitivity of the horse's mouth. Driving a four-in-hand can never be successful, if the mouth of one horse is soft and that of the other is hard, so that they do not rest equally on their bits. Hungarian bits have been created to eliminate these natural differences.

Bits can be efficient only if the reins are properly adjusted. The mere change of the bit is not enough to curb the horse.

When learning new exercises, some horses may need a stronger bit, and when they are already well-trained, they can be put back onto the original bit.

A very fine and lively relationship can be established between driver and horse by using Hungarian bits. Proper bits definitely play a major role in the successful performances of Hungarian carriages.

Parts and Function of a Hungarian Harness

There is no harness which fits all horses, and therefore the animals should be measured before harness-orders are placed. It is impossible to have a harness made for each and every horse, but one should be aware of the general size of the stock. Differences can be eliminated by adjustable buckling. There is no point in going into detail about measurements, since the different parts of a harness vary depending on the breed chosen for the eventing team. (Arab, Lipizaner, Nonius, Kisbér, Half-Bred or the Hungarian Half-Bred.)

Breast-Band

The transfer of traction and braking power takes place by means of the breast-band which should be made of strong, well-wrought, greasy oxhide. There is a chest-ring on the front where the bearing rein is buckled in, and on both ends there are the pull-ring (trace-clip), the pommel and the loops for the traces.

In event-coaches and style carriages the pull-ring is replaced by the so-called trace-clip. Experience shows that copper clips are not very durable because the pin easily deforms or even breaks, and therefore it is advisable to have the pin made of steel. Draught harnesses with rope

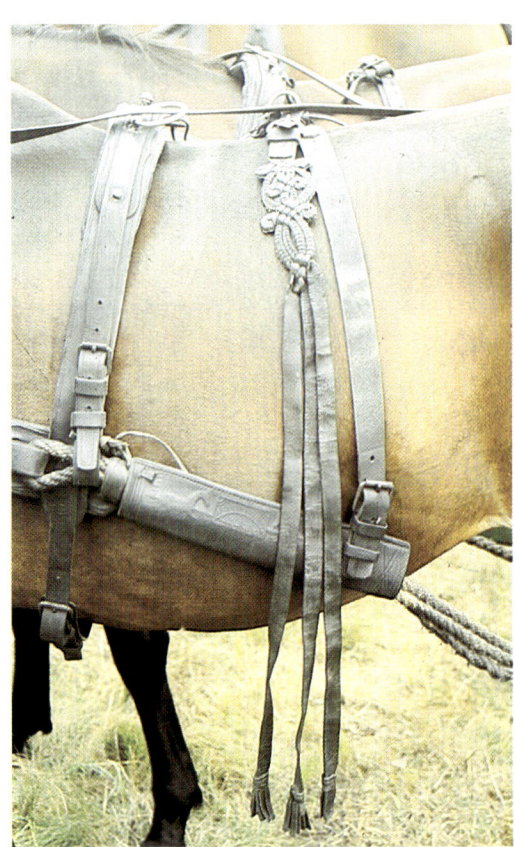

36 The decoration of a folk team, braided on top, cut at the bottom and ending in leather tassels. Traditional decoration from the area around Debrecen

solved this problem: they tie one knot on the off-reins and another on the near-reins, so that they are always readily able to adjust the length and do not have to fumble around, even after having taken a sharp turn.

Knotting reins is, of course, unknown in British dressage yet there is no objection to this in marathon and obstacle driving: i.e. it is permissible for the reins to be knotted.

We would like to mention a typical Hungarian rein, the "Széchenyi rein" used mainly in driving a carriage-and-pair, established and introduced more than 100 years ago by Dénes Széchenyi. The main point of the Széchenyi-rein is that the cross-straps of the double reins do not unite on both sides in one rein, but they

or chain traces still have a pull-ring. By fastening the traces to the ring, an unintentional knot may rub against the horse's flank. A so-called **trace-flap** pulled over the knot and the ring protects the horse's body. A style harness has the trace-clip on the lower extension of the breast-band, so that neither the clip nor the traces touch the horse which makes the trace-flap superfluous. Hungarian trace-loops are always bifurcated; pressed loops are not in accordance with Hungarian tradition.

Shoulder-Strap or the Withers-Strap

The fixing, the suspension and the adjustment of the breast-band is made by the shoulder-strap. It is very important to adjust it properly as, if it is put too high, it throttles the horse, and if it is too low, the withers of the horse can break. When walking downhill, the withers-strap takes the strain and not the neck-strap. One style harness, the "Cseklész" has an auxiliary neck-strap assisting the withers-strap.

The Hungarian training harness also has an auxiliary neck-strap, otherwise the withers-strap would be exposed to extreme pressure and would probably break under the strain.

There are harnesses with bifurcated shoulder-straps, but they are not original in style.

The rein terret is on the outside of the withers-strap. In a four-in-hand it is only the outside rein of the harnessed wheeler which is pulled through this terret, the leader's rein passes through the ear-ring of the bridle.

Back-Strap with Pommel and Girth

The back-strap has to hold the back of the breast-band and the harness as a whole. The pommel can be soft or hard.

Soft ones have the pommel-ring stitched on, hard ones have them screwed on. The pommel can be hardened by a steel plate. Most style harnesses are produced with hard pommels. (There are pommels covered with patent leather, however, they are not in accordance with Hungarian style.)

For a Hungarian pommel the same kind of leather should be used as for the other parts of the harness. There is no hook on top, but a simple screw called the "centre button".

37 Before the marathon sometimes ropes are mounted near the bearing rein. Such a harness lacks proper style and the bifurcated shoulder-strap is not typically Hungarian either

38 Carriage-horse in training harness just before being hitched to a vehicle

39 The four-in-hand of the Jászberény Stud: Cream Hungarian Half-Bred stallions in light Hungarian ornamental harness, hitched to a "Cziráky" carriage

Hungarian Harnesses

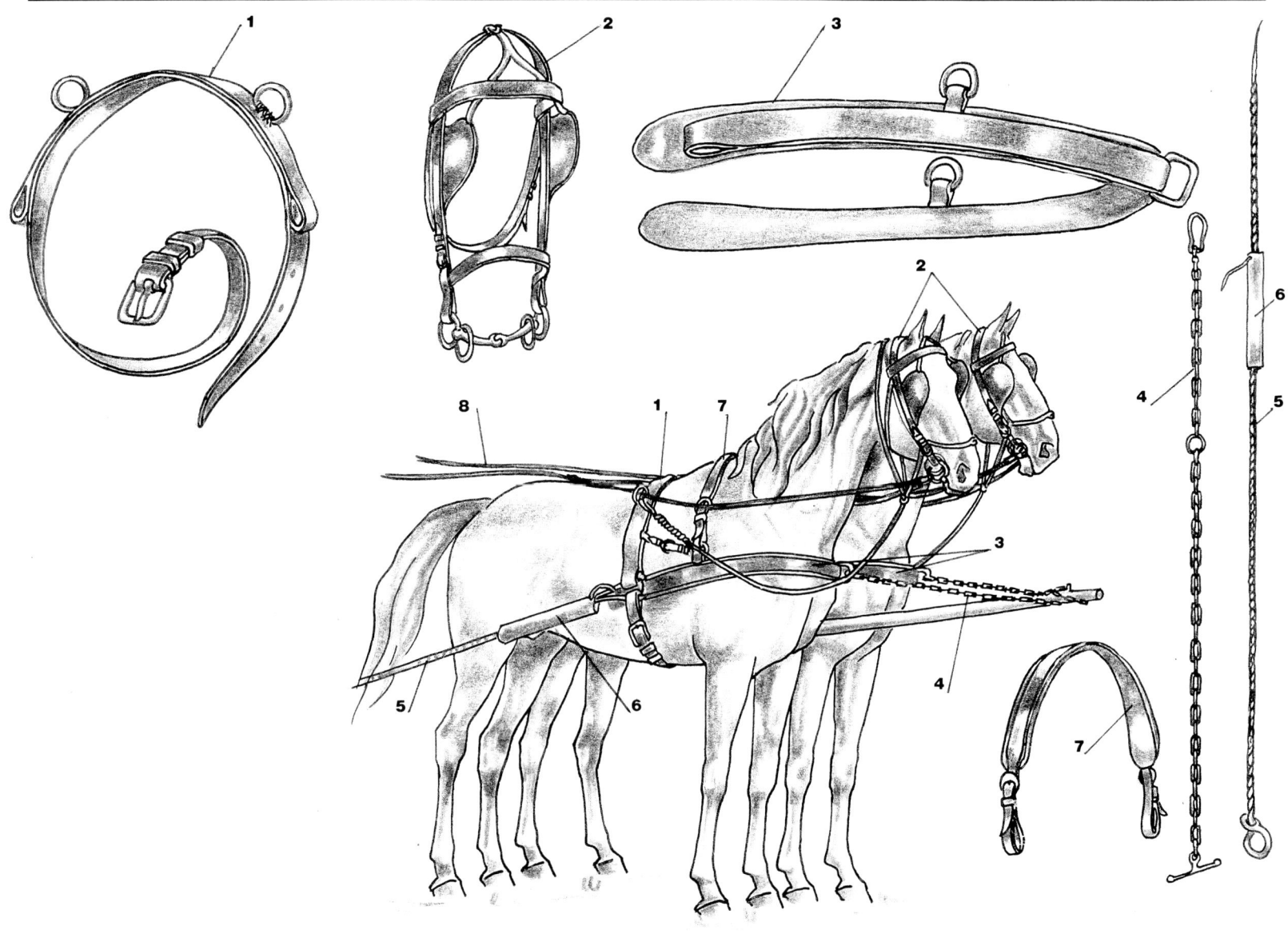

The parts of a draught-harness

1. Pommel (or back-strap) with girth
2. Bridle
3. Breast-band
4. Chain traces
5. Swingle-tree trace
6. Rope traces
7. Shoulder-strap or withers-strap
8. Chain support
9. Reins

Parts and Function of a Hungarian Harness 33

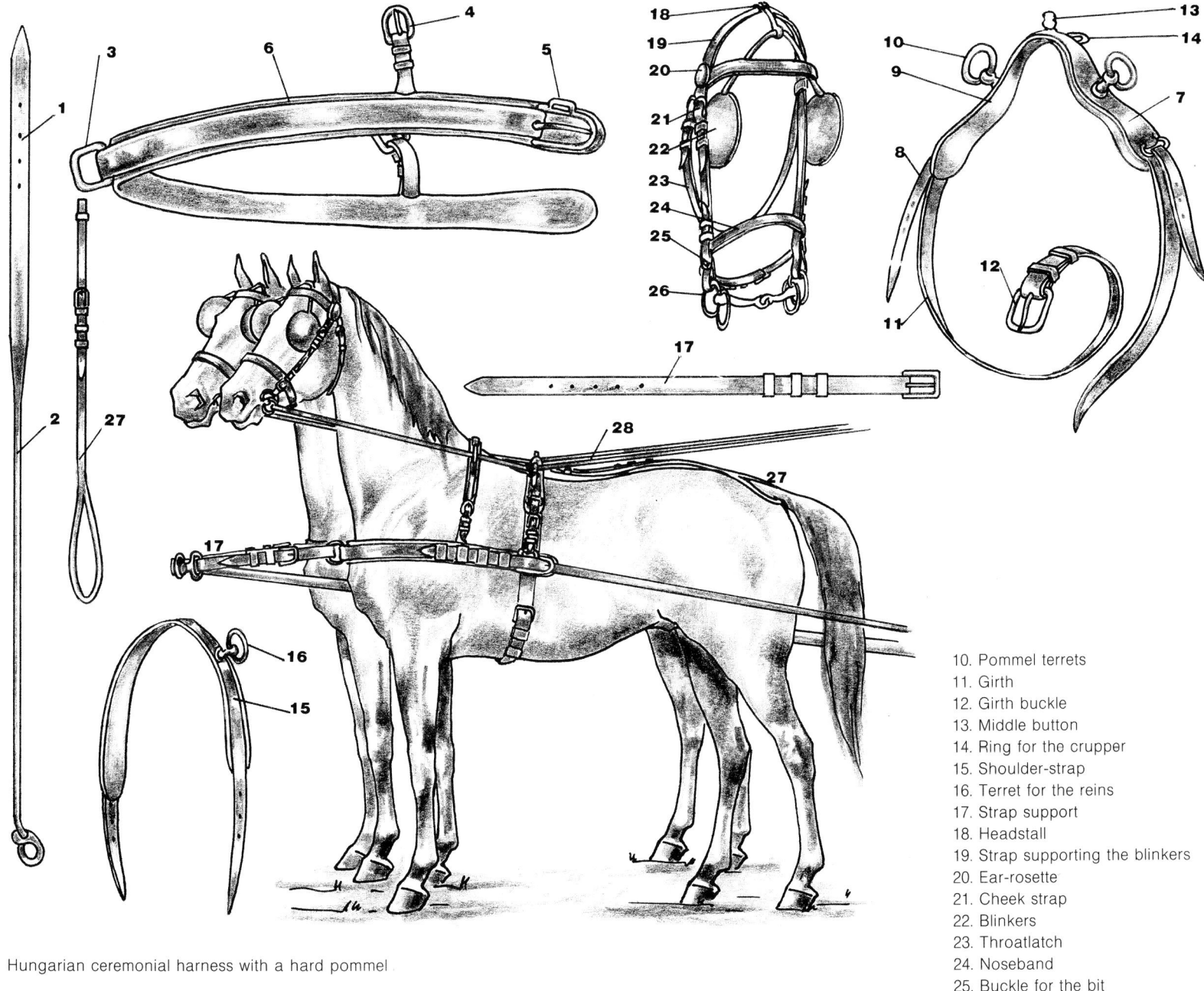

Hungarian ceremonial harness with a hard pommel.

1. Trace-buckle
2. Continuation of trace knotted at the end
3. Breast-ring
4. Shoulder-strap buckle
5. Buckle for the traces
6. Breast-band
7. Pommel
8. Pommel strap
9. Pommel pad
10. Pommel terrets
11. Girth
12. Girth buckle
13. Middle button
14. Ring for the crupper
15. Shoulder-strap
16. Terret for the reins
17. Strap support
18. Headstall
19. Strap supporting the blinkers
20. Ear-rosette
21. Cheek strap
22. Blinkers
23. Throatlatch
24. Noseband
25. Buckle for the bit
26. Bit
27. Crupper
28. Reins

A sweat-cloth is not used for a harness with a hard pommel. It would incur penalty points.

The pommel-rings are used for conducting the reins on one side. In a four-in-hand, besides the outer crossed reins, the leaders' reins on one side are also pulled through the pommel-ring. On both ends of the pommels there are small straps used for adjusting the height of the breast-band.

As the pommels are in the extension of the back-strap, they are connected to the girth which holds the whole harness. It would be wrong to believe that a carriage driving downhill should be held back by the girth. The shoulder-strap, the neck-strap, the back-strap and the pommel take over this function.

If the measurements are wrong, i.e. the breast-band is too short and the pole is too long, the girth and the girth-clip will slide forward and gall the horse's armpit. As in most cases only wheelers suffer from such chafing, non-experts may come to the conclusion that the animal often has to hold back the vehicle through the girth when hauling loads in hilly areas. This is unfortunately a very common occurrence, but easy to correct by taking the right measurements of the pole and of the breast-band.

The horses in a carriage-and-pair, as well as the wheelers of a four-in-hand do not need belly-bands, since the bearing rein (buckled into the spectacles on the pole-end) passes through the chest-ring and thus stops the breast-band sliding along the back-strap. The leaders, however, are not tied to the pole, and therefore do need a belly-band. Normal girth is buckled tighter than the auxiliary ones which are pulled over the pin of the trace-clip.

While measuring the length and buckling the belly-band, the closed clips should be at the same level.

The bells are fitted on the trace-clip at the point at which the girth, the back-strap and the breast-band join. Either all the horses have a bell or none of them. A four-in-hand always has bells, while a carriage-and-pair, like horse-drawn sledges, needs them only in winter. Competitive four-in-hands have bells mounted for parades, cavalcades and dressage. Bells are not

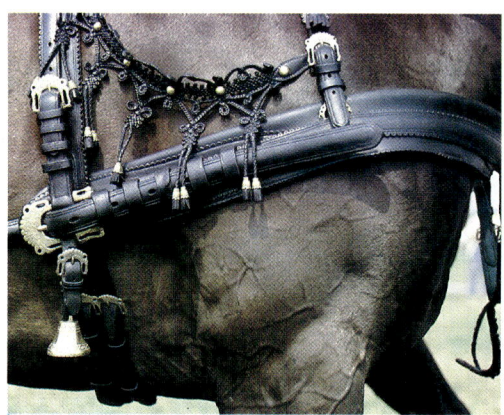

40 The auxiliary belly-band buckled properly on the leaders of a four-in-hand. The bell is also correctly fitted

obligatory but they are definitely of advantage, especially if they ring harmoniously in tune.

Usually the owner's coat of arms or initials are put on the blinkers and on the pommels. Nowadays, instead of initials and coats of arms one can only see a meaningless stamp which is poor even as a form of decoration.

In state studs new branding signs indicating the different studs have been designed. These resemble initials and, if made of copper, are attractive and, besides, they do have a meaning. Riding schools have no studs of their own, but of course, their teams can use the coat of arms of the Hungarian People's Republic. Hungarian teams selected for international events should also bear the coat of arms of the State. The initiatives at Bábolna, Mezőhegyes and Szilvásvárad are highly appreciated, and so their teams wear the stud-seal on the pommel and on the blinkers of the harness.

All of this may demonstrate the good taste and care of the owner.

We have already mentioned the small screw on the pommel, the "centre button". Instead of that, many harnesses have a hook having no special function, but amateurs like to use it to decorate their carriages. (The hook has a certain function on trotter harness: the check-rein supporting the horse's head is fastened to this hook.) One should never confuse a trotter with a carriage harness.

Traces

Traces can be made of: hemp-rope, chain, leather or leather-coated rope.

The hemp-rope traces are in general used for cross-country events (chain traces only occasionally) as they can be easily cut if the carriage overturns or the horse slips. Chain traces are rather difficult to loosen, can cause injuries and rattle awfully. They are mainly used for draught carriages, flat vehicles with pneumatic tires and for heavy-duty ferry horses.

Leather or leather-covered rope traces are used for carriage-driving. They are practical, easily adjustable and removable as well as durable. They are just as flexible as rope traces but look nicer.

Traces made of pure leather are always flat. Their production does not need any special skill. In style, flat traces match only the collar-harness, but they are, nonetheless, more widely spread. Flat traces are suitable mainly for cross-country harness and for training.

Traditionalists often criticize flat as being liable to twine around the whipple-tree at an angle of 90°, so that their edges are against the horse and rub the animal's skin. However, experience clearly refutes this theory showing that the flat traces make only half a twist while turning only a part of the edge against the horse and, if the edge-corners are properly rounded, they cannot do any harm to the animal.

Hungarian ceremonial harnesses are not allowed to use other than leather-covered rope traces. The rope can be covered by stitched plain leather or by leather braid. The making of braided traces requires a great deal of skill and time, and that is the reason why they are quite expensive. The price, however, should not discourage anybody, as these traces are well worth buying. In general there can be no objection to traces covered by plain leather, but once they are worn out they should be replaced by braided ones. Leather-covered rope traces are not so long-lasting as leather-made flat traces, and they should be used only for ceremonial harness.

It is always difficult to take the right measurements of the pole and of the traces: the main point is that they should fit harness-horses.

Sledges need specially made traces which are 15–20 cm longer. It should be taken into consideration that today's horses are taller and sturdier and of stronger frames than those of fifty years ago and so the measurements of that time are no longer valid.

A short survey follows on current trace sizes. (The figures refer to the length between the knob on the swingle-tree and the trace-clip's end.)

For the wheelers in a four-in-hand
and a carriage-and-pair .... 190–205 cm
For sledges .... 205–220 cm
For the leaders
in a four-in-hand .... 180–190 cm

Trace length is of special importance as the manoeuvrability of the carriage depends on this.

Bridle

The main parts of the bridle are:
— headstall and cheek straps
— browband
— the blinkers and their holder with straps
— throatlatch
— noseband
— bit

The most eye-catching are the blinkers which are always rounded off on Hungarian bridles and bear a coat of arms or some other special insignia.

The cheek straps and the noseband are adjustable, but it must be emphasized again that horses should be measured properly before having a harness made, as no bridle would fit both the head of an Arab mare and that of a Half-Bred stallion from a Hanover crossing.

If the noseband, the browband and the joints are loose, this not only gives a bad impression but hinders the horse in its performance.

The browband is generally decorated with a star, a metal stud or a chain. The metal front is unusual on Hungarian harnesses and because it cannot lie close enough on the horse's head it disturbs the animal; therefore it cannot be even recommended for training.

On the noseband of a Hungarian bridle there are two loops used to fasten the straps which hold the bit. The noseband should be fitted neither too tightly nor too loosely. (If it is too loose, the bridle does not sit firmly and this disturbs the horse.) The noseband can be buckled more tightly if an increased bit-effect is required, however, a thin auxiliary nose-strap (nose-brake) does just as well, especially for horses which hold the bit too firmly.

The "nose-brake" is more efficient if it is buckled onto the bit-ring rather than if it is fixed to the ring suspending the bit.

For training, instead of the noseband, Hungarian drivers often use simple cords (as used for tying bales) which are just as good as nosebands made by a saddler, although they still offend good taste.

The next accessory of the bridle is the bit; the subject of much discussion among drivers. We shall discuss the bits that have proved by experience to be the most suitable, and are still used by prominent Hungarian drivers. As mentioned before, all the horses in a competitive carriage should rest equally on their bits, otherwise the whole team cannot perform efficiently (especially when turning quickly or changing pace suddenly). Even the horses of well-trained teams show a different degree of sensitivity in their mouths, which can be compensated by using the appropriate bits.

Proper skill is needed to select and apply bits as the wrong ones can harm the horse and reduce its abilities. It is always up to the driver to decide for how long he applies a certain bit. New exercises may make the horse press against the bit too heavily, in which case the driver has to apply a stronger bit to keep the animal under

41 The four-horse sledge of the Nagycenk State Stud driving out for a winter hunt. When hitching the horses to a sledge, the traces of the wheelers should be lengthened by 15 to 20 cm or replaced by longer ones

better control. However, after a few days (sometimes after only a few hours) the horse should be given back its original, lighter bit.

With the following kinds of bits all new training exercises can easily be carried out:
— foal bit
— bar bit
— rubber bar bit
— twisted bar bit
— double-jointed twisted bit.

The order in which these bits are listed reflects their sharpness—the last one being the sharpest. The rubber one is used mainly for medical therapy. The foal bit is the most popular in Hungary. Its sharpness is adjustable by varying the thickness at the edge of the horse's mouth. The thicker the bit the less sharp it is. The four-ring jointed foal bit is considered to be an ancient Hungarian bit; the precursor of all other bits. Its inventor is unknown, but the fact is that it appeared contemporaneously to regular carriage-driving in response to increased demands.

Previously, the use of bits stronger than the foal bit was not encouraged by the management of equestrian sports in Hungary. Today, all the above mentioned bits are allowed. These bits with their four rings look like the foal bit.

As the name implies, foals should have a foal bit for their first exercises. This bit should be at least the thickness of a man's thumb and on no account thin and sharp. A horse trained professionally with a foal bit will seldom need a stronger one later.

Before changing a bit, try first to give the horse an auxiliary nose-strap and, only if it does not bring the expected result, should stronger bit be applied.

The leading reins may be buckled onto both bit-rings for two reasons: 1. in order to reduce the bit's restraining effect or 2. to prevent the horse from turning the bit in its mouth and thus twisting the reins.

By buckling the reins onto both bit-rings, the sharpness of some bits can be adjusted, which means that one and the same bit can be made more or less sharp. This is quite a remarkable advantage in the refinement phase of training.

A simple twisted bit and a double-jointed

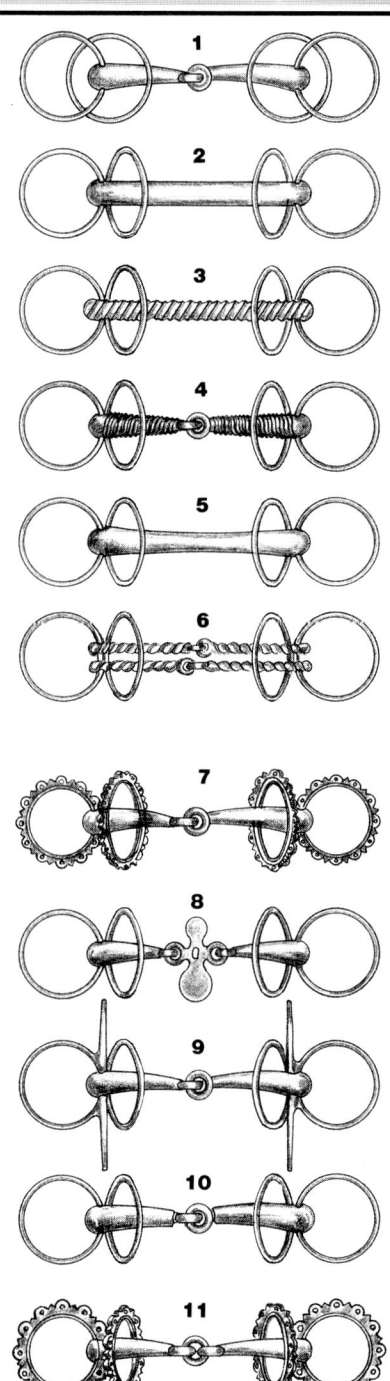

twisted bit should never be used, except as a last resort when no result can be achieved by using a bar bit together with a nose-strap (nose-brake).

Nowadays, drivers often have to buy the horses for their teams themselves. The mouths of those which have been trained by other people may be in a bad condition. Therefore, when buying a horse the first thing to do is to check the condition of the mouth. If the mouth is sore because of fretting the bit the horse should be given a rubber bit at first until the sores heal. The rubber bit may never have to be replaced by a sharper one, but if the rubber bit and the nose-strap do not help, a sharper bit is unavoidable.

In a team of mares one of the animals may start rutting. A rutting mare is generally sluggish, but occasionally it may become oversensitive and start to gallop. In this case a temporary nose-strap or a stronger, sharper bit will help. Professionally trained harness-horses are generally easy to drive with a foal bit, and therefore every driver should try to train his horses in this way.

Leading Reins

This too is a very important part of the harness. The British art of carriage-driving differs from the Hungarian in the way the reins are fastened. In Hungary a "frog" is used.

The colour of Hungarian reins is always that of untreated yellow leather and care should be taken to prevent them from becoming black.

Drivers of a carriage-and-pair prefer the so-called French rein (mentioned as "Széchenyi

The different bits used by Hungarian drivers
1. Simple-jointed four-ring bit
2. Bar bit
3. Twisted bar bit with four rings
4. Simple-jointed twisted bit
5. Rubber bit with steel chain
6. Double-jointed twisted bit
7. Simple-jointed ornamental four-ring bit
8. Bit with spoon-like mouthpiece
9. Simple-jointed bit with rods
10. Jointed four-ring bit covered with rubber
11. Jointed four-ring play-bit

rein" by Sándor Pettkó after the name of its inventor, Dénes Széchenyi), as it is the most suitable for exact adjustments. The method of buckling makes it possible to change the horse's position both backwards and forwards depending on the drawing power required. French reins can be a help in correcting animals that tend to move obliquely or to one side.

The reins of a carriage-and-pair may be considered well-adjusted when the heads of the horses deviate only slightly from the pole.

Draught teams and parade coaches still have crossed reins which do not permit exact adjustment. As horses for a four-in-hand are always trained first in a carriage-and-pair, the French reins are indispensable for training for both types of carriages.

Four-in-hands have in general crossed reins, the leading reins continuing where the reins cross upon the leaders and those upon the wheelers converge in the frog in the driver's hand. A driver with large hands holds the frog in his hands, while a small-handed person holds the reins in front of the frog. The frog should be adjusted in such a way that it enables the driver to sit up straight and to hold the reins with bent arms. The frog is used for putting the horses either into the position for moving straight ahead or for pulling. If the leaders are required to stop pulling, the leading reins have to be shortened by means of the frog.

A very frequent mistake is to pull the reins of the leaders through the terrets on the withers-straps of the wheelers. When putting together a four-in-hand, it is unnecessary to pull the reins of the leaders through the terret on the withers-strap since there is a special rein-ring fitted on a 10–15 cm long strap suspended on the rosette of the wheelers' bridles. Therefore, the reins of the leaders should be pulled only through the pommel-ring and through the above-mentioned rein-ring. Reins pulled through the withers-terret might break and thus make the carriage difficult to manœuvre.

Reins are generally sold with ready-made holes, and only the first drive can reveal whether the holes are in the right places or not. If not, new holes have to be punched. This can spoil the appearance and weaken the rein. Therefore, it is advisable to buy new, unpierced French reins. A punch which is adjustable to the different hole-sizes is as important to a racing team as any other part of the equipment, since it can be used for punching holes in the other, older, stretched reins as well.

The driver should hold the new, unpunched reins with bent arms, sit straight up and allow the team to trot. The first basic holes should then be made at the exact point where the driver holds the rein, sitting comfortably and keeping the horses' heads deviating slightly outwards. However, the holes can be punched 2 to 3 cm further forward to allow for stretching.

The next step is to punch four extra holes both in front and behind the principal hole. The rein has then nine holes providing enough possibilities for adjustment.

Generally only one hole is made where the rein is connected to the bit, but sometimes there

42 Properly fitted leading rein

are even two to adjust the length of the reins buckled upon both bit-rings. The reins are sometimes buckled onto two rings only on one side (the pole-side) thus shortening the inside rein, and this pulls the horse's head inwards. In this case, not the frog has to be readjusted, but the second hole near the bit-ring should be used to give the rein the required length which produces the same result as buckling the reins onto one ring. More than two holes at the bit-buckle are unnecessary.

Where the reins cross there is a ring which is not attached but holds the reins in position. This ring is made of ivory or deer-horn; both of these materials look very elegant, but if they are not available, a studded metal ring will do just as well. The cross-reins of a four-in-hand are more complicated and require more practice and care to ensure that they are properly adjusted. By lengthening the outside rein of the crossed reins the inside rein will be proportionally shortened and vice versa. A very clever technique is to punch the first holes in such a way that the difference in size and the length of the inside and outside reins are the same for both the cross-reins and the French reins. Thus, even when using the cross-reins, the horses will not change the position of their heads. The cross-reins do not need more than two additional holes above and below to allow for adjustment. The first hole on the reins of a four-in-hand should be made at the frog where the reins of the leaders and wheelers cross and where it seems obviously necessary to the driver, when he is sitting properly and the horses are pulling the carriage at a trot. When harnessing, the cross-reins of the leaders often get mixed up, and therefore a cross or a metal button is usually put on the ends of the cross-reins to prevent this.

In the same way as for the French rein, every four holes should be punched every 4 cm above and below the basic hole. As stretching is possible, buckles should be fitted only on the rein-ends of the wheelers, while the reins of the leaders end in a keeper behind the frog, and are 20 cm shorter than those of the wheelers. Thus the keeper ensures that both reins are always flat on top of each other. The end of the rein is

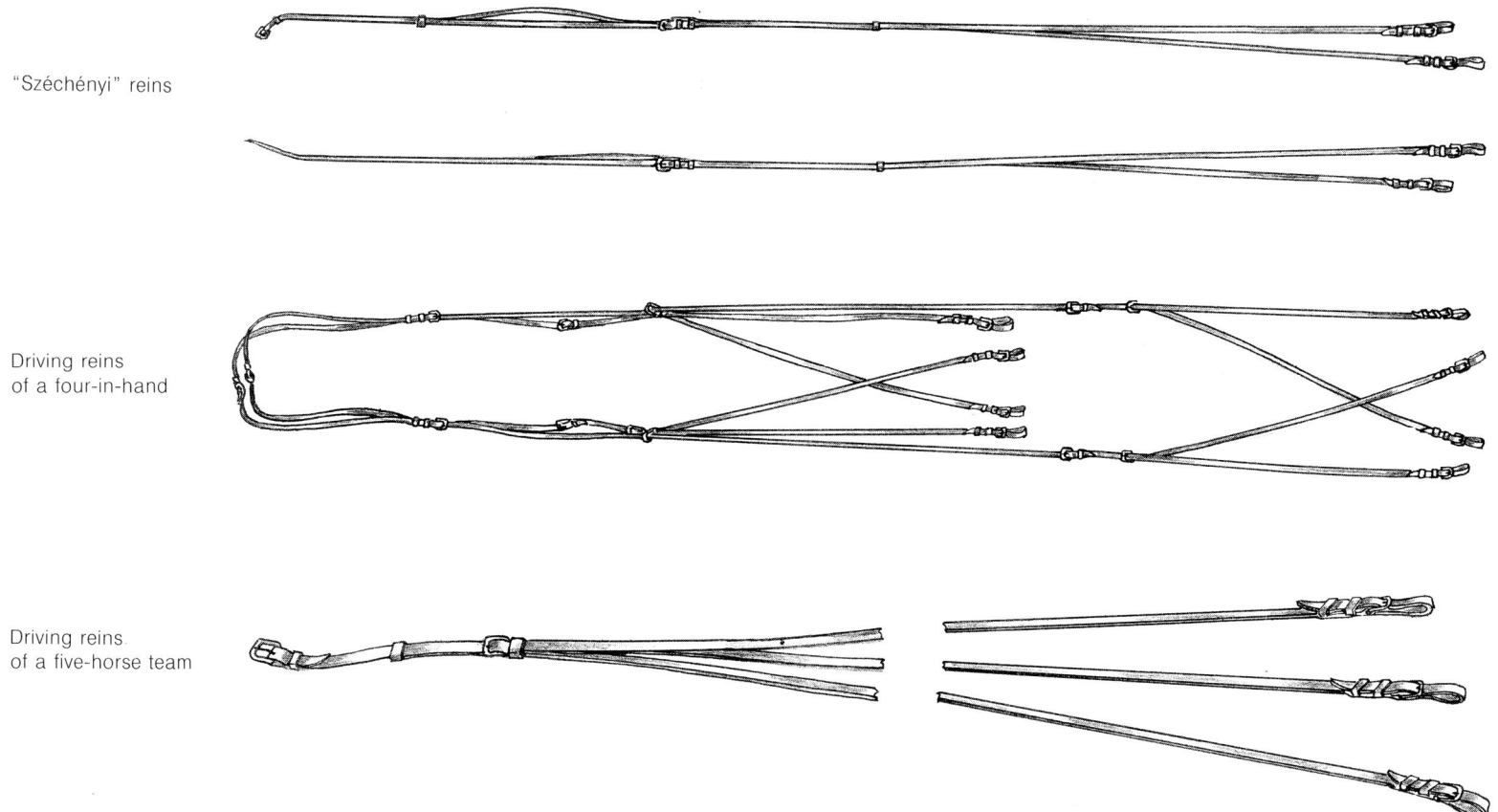

"Széchényi" reins

Driving reins of a four-in-hand

Driving reins of a five-horse team

attached either to the back of the front seat or to a looped strap fixed to the seat-board behind the seat-padding. These methods are both functional and attractive.

Crupper

The crupper serves to fasten the caparison on the side as well as the strap supporting the traces. It should be neither too tight nor too loose. When buckling the crupper care must be taken not to let the end of the clip project, because the cross-reins could get caught in it. It is best to adjust only the lower strap leaving the upper one as it is. The caparison should be so attached to the crupper that it lies exactly between the withers and the flanks. The straps supporting the traces should lie on the barrel.

Neck-Strap

On draught harnesses there is a separate neck-strap attached to the pole-end by a chain support. The horses use it when going downhill to hold back the carriage.

A neck-strap does not usually belong to style harness, but it is advisable to put one on cross-country and training harnesses as it relieves the shoulder-strap on steep hills, in ditches, and when sudden stops are made. In a four-in-hand, only the wheelers need, of course, an auxiliary neck-strap as it is they who hold back the carriage. Sometimes the leaders may have one as well to match the others, although it has no practical use.

The auxiliary neck-strap is pulled through the leather loop stitched on top of the shoulder-strap. At one end there is a half-ring through which the bearing-rein passes. A buckle and a loop allow the neck-strap to be adjusted in size. The auxiliary neck-strap can be pulled in and out of this loop.

Nowadays, more and more style carriages have an auxiliary neck-strap for obstacle driving, as it lightens the burden on the weak shoulder-strap, especially when sudden stops or changes of pace are made. It is still a subject for discussion whether the auxiliary neck-strap should be allowed in competitions or not. Undoubtedly, most style harnesses have been designed for parades in which they are not exposed to very much strain, but such pleasure-driving cannot be compared to a driving competition in which the auxiliary neck-strap

Bearing Rein and Connecting Strap

matching the style of the harness is a strict requirement.

Ornamental neck-straps, usually ending in a leather tassel, have no other function but that of being decorative. In winter, and on sledges, the ceremonial neck-strap may have a bell attached.

The wheelers of a four-in-hand have so-called bearing reins for holding back the vehicle. These reins pass through the breast-ring and the half-ring of the neck-strap as well as through the spectacles on the pole-end. Strong ones are made of double-stitched and double-thick oxhide. A frequent mistake is to have brass buckles with brass tongues which break easily. Steel tongues are much stronger and thus save the driver a lot of trouble.

In order to prevent the horses from moving apart, a connecting strap is buckled into the breast-rings of the leaders. This is typical of

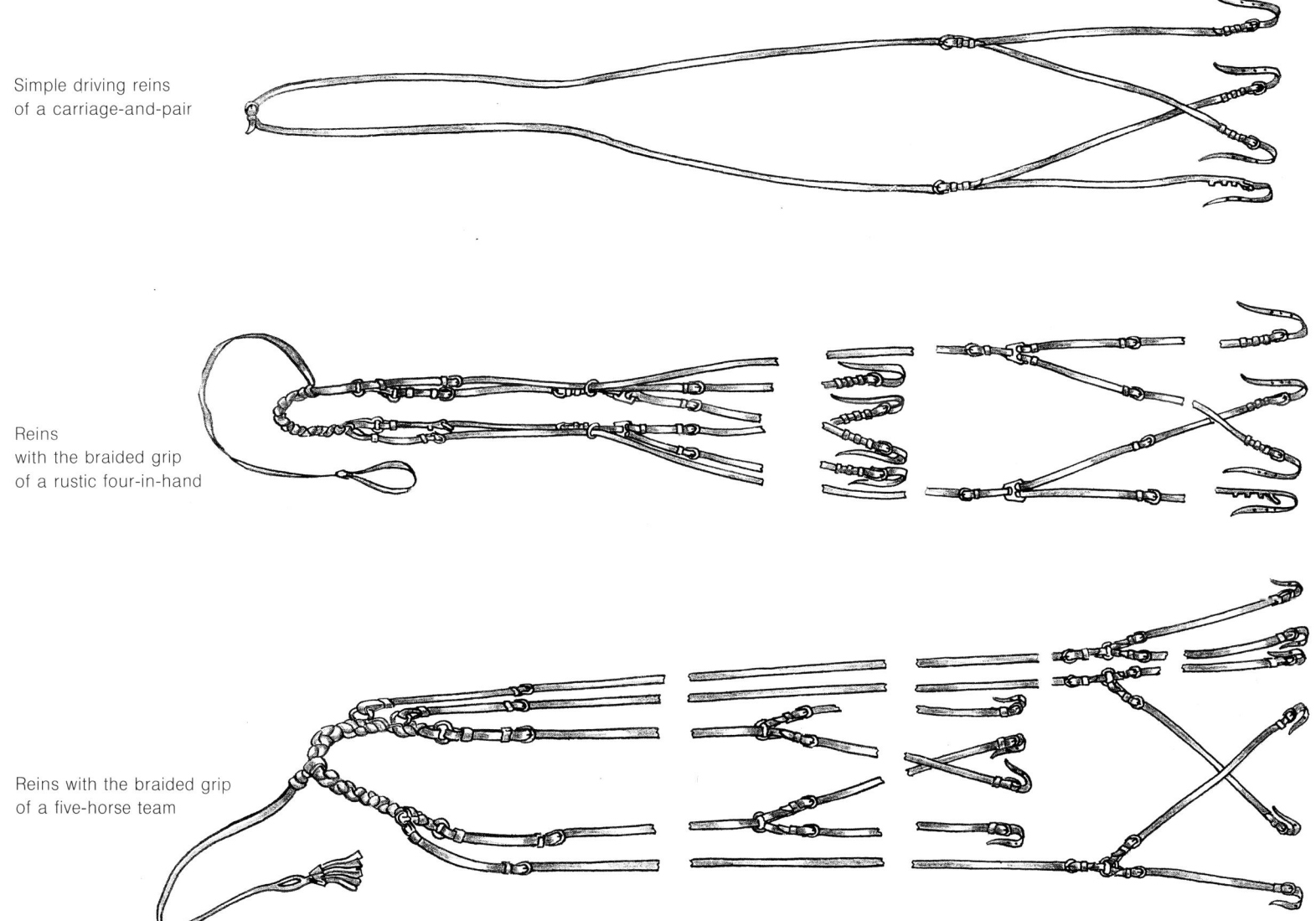

Simple driving reins of a carriage-and-pair

Reins with the braided grip of a rustic four-in-hand

Reins with the braided grip of a five-horse team

Hungarian harnessing. Its shape, the studdings and the way the connecting strap is attached are completely in keeping with the other fittings of the harness. (British teams do not usually have a connecting strap.) However, more and more British drivers now use one to permit better acceleration.

The connecting strap should not be too tight, otherwise the horses may trample on each other's legs and cause injuries.

Harness Decorations

Leather caparisons and textile butterflies belong quite naturally to a Hungarian harness, but there are harnesses without decoration of any kind.

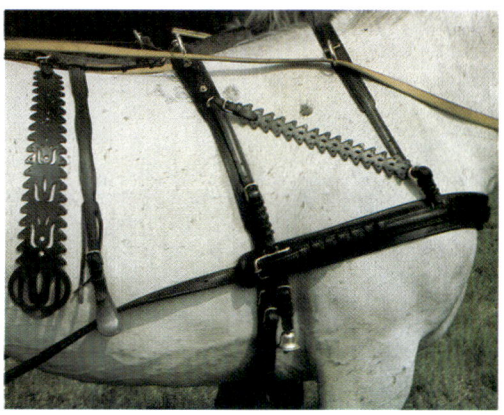

43 Hungarian harness with openwork decoration and plain studding

The original function of the caparison was to protect the horses from flies.

The caparison can be: skived, braided or openworked. There are bridle-caparisons and back caparisons for the different parts of the horse's body.

The textile butterflies are made of cloth. Although they can be combined with caparisons, some harnesses have no other decoration.

Drivers and team-owners with good taste always use textile in colours matching the carriage covers. On style harnesses the textile butterflies serve only as complementary decoration; the main ornaments are the leather caparisons.

44 Light Hungarian ornamental harness.
The rein which leads to the front horses is pulled through the shoulder ring the wrong way and it will obviously break

45 This is an unusual way of fitting the front decoration by buckles; it is generally stiltched to the browband

Parts and Function of a Hungarian Harness

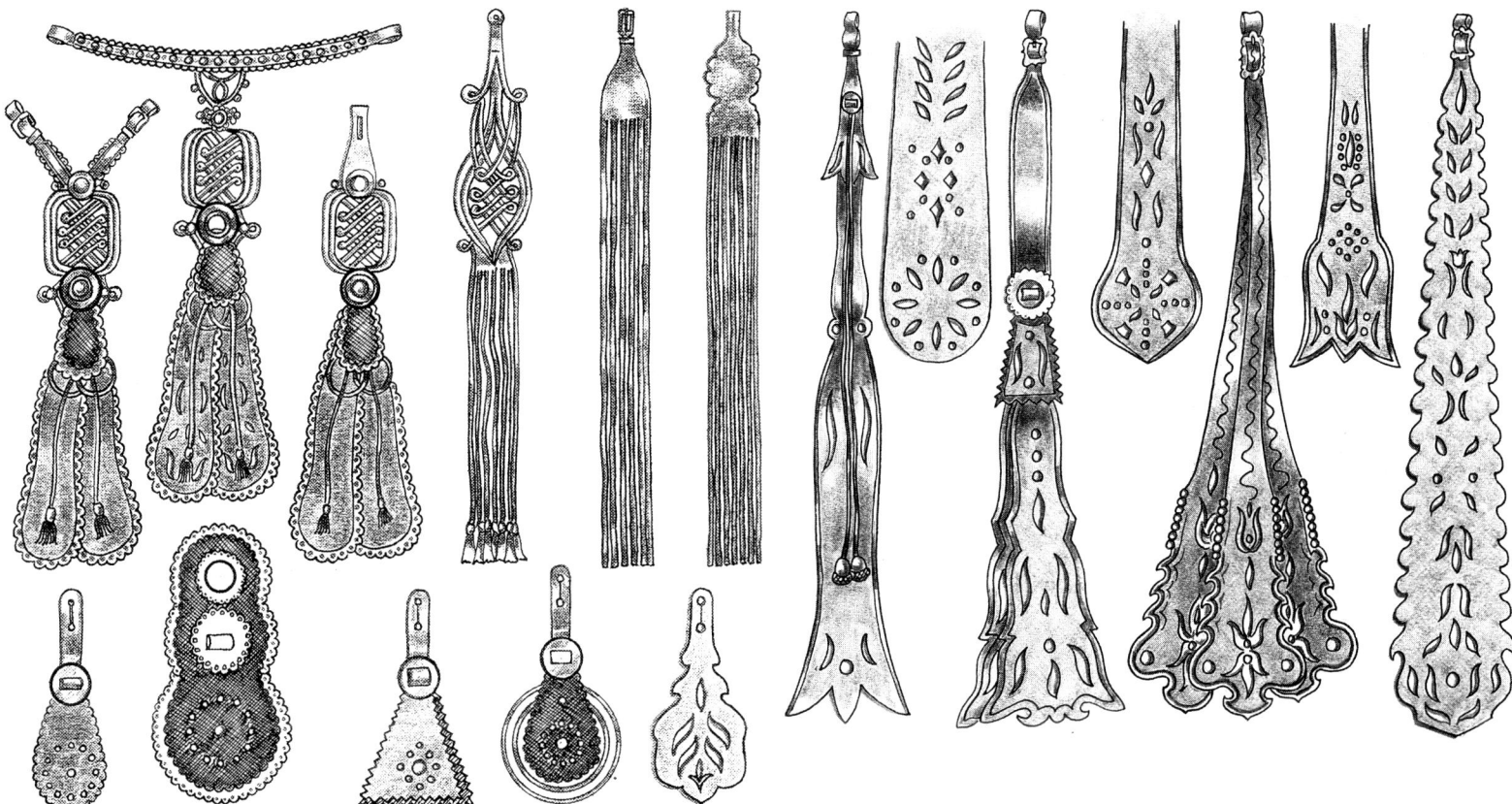

Various "butterflies" made of cloth or leather

Different kinds of leather decorations: bounds, skived or openwork

Different openwork motifs on decorative leather caparisons

The horses of a carriage-and-pair, as well as the wheelers of a four-in-hand have two kinds of leather decorations on their bridles: one is stitched onto the browband, and the other pulled through the outer rosette. There is no leatherwork under the rosette on the pole-side. At the same time the leaders of a four-in-hand have leather decorations under both rosettes and on the browband.

The back caparison is placed on properly only if it lies on the mid-line between the pommel and the horse's flank. A heavy ornamental harness can have even two back caparisons which should be placed on top of each other proportionally. Care must be taken not to allow the caparisons to slide under the traces.

The caparison should match in colour the harness as a whole. Besides the textile butterflies, metal studs, stars and rings may be used to decorate the caparison, but the material should harmonize with the other ornamental elements.

The most decorative caparisons are those which are braided. They should always have notched studding.

A caparison with openwork matches a harness with plain studs made of non-ferrous metal best. Ethnographers trace back the origin of the openwork patterns to the symbolizing of the shaman world in ancient Hungarian mythology.

Skived caparisons, being simple, suit rustic vehicles best.

Of the decorative parts of a harness the kidney-strap also merits to be mentioned. One end is tied into the half-ring on the bottom end of the pommel, the other is fastened to the buckle connecting the shoulder-strap to the breast-band (in the region of the shoulder-blade). The kidney-strap has no practical use, although it had a function on ancient, simple harnesses consisting merely of a breast-band, two traces and a pommel without a girth. Kidney-straps are braided and decorated with leather tassels and other metal ornamentation. A Hungarian ceremonial harness with notched stud should not lack a kidney-strap.

Under the event-rules, teams have to be equipped in the same way in dressage as in obstacle driving. This is a problem for some drivers, as horses may be disturbed by the ca-

Hungarian Harnesses

Braided leather decorations

parison or other decorations and toss their heads all the time. The only way to avoid this is to train with trappings. Simple decorations will suffice for training, but the size should be in accord with those of the ceremonial harness. Wearing trappings all the time, the horses will get accustomed to them and find them natural in all situations.

Horses like to champ on the leather decorations, which is another problem. Gnawn leather is rather ugly and difficult to repair. Horses can be weaned from the habit of gnawing by smearing the leather parts with rabbit or pig gall.

Studding and Bells

Studs can be of non-ferrous metal (the simplest is brass) or of nickel, nickel-alloy or, but this is rather seldom, of silver.

Simple harnesses have black painted metal rings and buckles. Buckles made of non-ferrous metal can be notched or plain, iron buckles are always plain. Though harnesses decorated with openwork and studs may be variously designed, they are all Hungarian in character.

It offends good style if both patterned and plain studding are combined. Trappings are allowed to have plain metal studs even if the buckles are notched. Studs make for a simple, braided trapping and for a more decorative appearance.

Besides the decorative studs, the owner's initials and coat of arms, which may be put on the blinkers and the pommels, have to be mentioned. The best are those indicating the stud or the club to which the team belongs. Military units and the Hungarian National Team are obliged to wear the coat of arms of the Hungarian People's Republic. The initials and coat of arms are made of the same material as the rest of the studding.

Skived leather decorations are mainly used for plain harnesses or for those which have patterned studs made of non-ferrous metal.

Bells attached to the loop on trace ends have always been used in Upper Northern Hungary (the northern part of the country before 1920), in Sub-Carpathia and in Transdanubia (the part of Hungary that lies between the Danube and the western frontier), while in the area surrounding Debrecen a big bell suspended on the horse's neck was popular.

This latter kind of bell can be seen now only in exhibitions. Today's competitive teams have, without exception, bells attached to the traces. Ethnographers unanimously maintain that

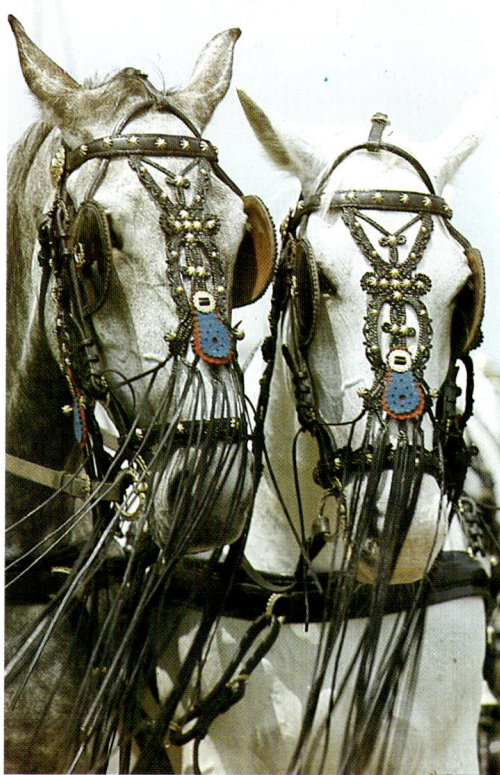

46 The light Hungarian ornamental harness is decorated with brass stars and rings as well as with clothmade "butterflies"

The Most Popular Hungarian Harnesses

Hungarian bells

Eastern nations used rattles. According to the findings of tomb-relics the general use of the rattle began in the 16th century, influenced by Western fashion.

To sit in a horse-drawn sledge equipped with rattles and bells in a snowy landscape, is a delightful and unforgettable experience.

The Most Popular Hungarian Harnesses

Hungarian harnesses are best classified according to their ornamentation. The variety is great and we shall present those that are most widely spread and which truly preserve tradition.

"Cseklész" Harness

This is one of the simplest among patterned Hungarian ceremonial harnesses and yet, nonetheless, fine and elegant with a practical design. The very first was used by the coachmen of the Esterházy family. The "Cseklész" harness forms an intermediate type between ceremonial and everyday harnesses.

The pommel is soft and both the pommel-rings and the shoulder-terrets are stitched on. The buckles and the rings are notched. A harness having both plain and ornamental studding does not look nice and gives the impression of artificial simplicity. Apart from the studding, there is skiver decoration on both the withers-strap and the loin-strap, as well as fringes on the nosebands and browbands.

47 The attachment of the bridle decoration. The front decoration is stitched to the browband. The ear-decoration is hung onto the ring of the rosette

48 The fitting of the openwork decoration onto the bridle

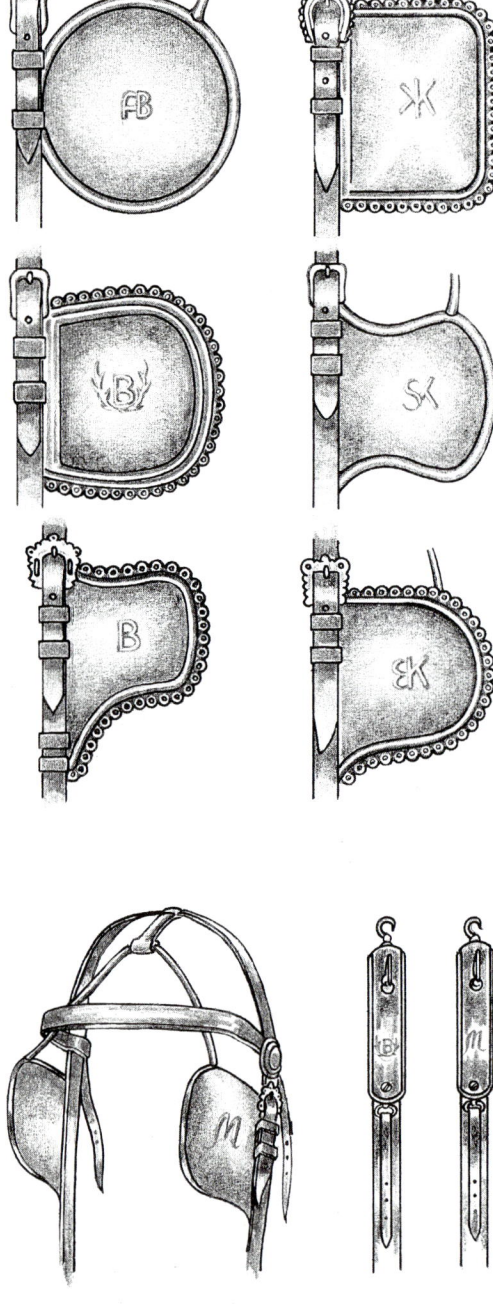

Various blinkers and ways of applying initials

The rosettes are decorated with large, bi-coloured butterflies made of cloth. Further ornaments are the **csülökbontó** (used to serve once for detaching the traces from the whipple-tree) made of deer-horn and attached to the loin-strap, as well as a brass comb for the mane and tail. The traces are normally covered with rounded leather, but there are flat strap-traces as well. This type of harness always has an auxiliary neck-strap.

Harness with Metal Studs

It is very similar to the simple "Cseklész" harness. The inventor is considered to be Imre Micski, lieutenant colonel of the Debrecen stud. The rings and the buckles are plain, the browband, the neck-strap, the kidney-strap, the loin-strap and the ceremonial neck-strap with a red tassel are densely studded (the studs are plain with a diameter of about one cm). The harness has flat strap-traces. Further attachments are the **csülökbontó** (mentioned above) made of deer-horn and the brass comb for the mane and tail. These are attached to the loin-strap.

Light Hungarian Ceremonial Harness with Decorative Studding

This is probably the closest to the ideal. Practical, light and elegant, it really meets all criteria.

The studs, buckles and rings are patterned and very finely wrought. Other ornamentation

49 The correct way of attaching the side decoration and the kidney-strap

includes the braided, light caparisons with metal studs and textile butterflies. There is a hard pommel to which the pommel-rings are stitched. The shoulder-straps and loin-straps are decorated with skiver.

This is definitely the most popular harness for carriage-driving competitions and, for a long time, it has been considered abroad to be the only Hungarian harness. The fact is that this harness does allow for many variations without losing its Hungarian character and individuality.

Heavy Hungarian Ceremonial Harness with Decorative Studding

This harness has very large studs, buckles and rings and, apart from the notched patterns, carved motifs serve as decoration. The caparisons are wide, long and rich. Sometimes there are even two caparisons for the side. It looks quite decorative on big horses like Half-Bred or Nonius stallions, but it nearly dwarfs the Arab, the Lipizaner and the Kisbér Half-Bred.

Some regional types have the straps on the breast, shoulder and back decorated with coloured leather which resembles needlework. The most beautiful harness is that of the five-horse carriage of the town of Debrecen, exhibited in the Hungarian Agricultural Museum. The red and green needlework shows a pattern of leaves and tulips.

Hungarian Ceremonial Harness with Fretwork Decoration

This is basically the same as the "Cseklész" harness, but the studding can be either plain or patterned. The pommel is, in most cases, soft.

The withers-strap and the loin-strap are decorated with skiver. Various additions are possible. Some harnesses have only decoration for the ears and not for the brow of the horse, although they have a braided crossed noseband on the bridle. In other cases, the noseband is plain, but there is an additional decoration of the brows.

The ear-fringes are usually long and hang down onto the breast-band. Shorter ear-fringes do not look quite as attractive. A kidney-strap which is cut in the style of the trappings as a whole can be put on as well. Only one caparison for the back and one for the side belong to the harness, but two of each—a big and a small one —can be used as well.

How the rein-leading ring on the wheelers of a four-in-hand is mounted. The buckle on the strap attached to the leading rein (drawing to the extreme right) can be a danger as it may get stuck. Different ways of attaching the crupper

Hungarian Harnesses

50 Braided decoration on the bridle with metal studs

51 The "butterfly" on the bridle of the "Cseklész" harness

This kind of decoration allows for individual taste and personal phantasy to produce a great number of different variations. This harness never has metal adornments, but it can be decorated with a ceremonial neck-strap with leather tassel.

The motifs are most traditional, and the harness is good for any breed and size of horse.

"Pozsony" Harness

This is a kind of light Hungarian ceremonial harness made of yellow leather. One is in the possession of the Bábolna Agricultural Complex. It looks very attractive especially on chestnut and black horses. Only its maintenance is a problem, as natural leather soon loses its original colour and water makes it brown and dark. This is the main reason why the "Pozsony" harness is not so popular.

"Jukker" Harness

This harness appeared in Hungary during the last century and has gained ground through the increasing popularity of marathon events. It is simple and practical without any decoration. The studs are plain and made of brass, nickel-alloy or silver. Although a "Jukker" harness with brass studding could have additional open-work decoration, this would be superfluous on a nickel or silver-studded "Jukker". Braided ornamentation does not suit this harness at all.

Easy maintenance and the ability to bear

52 Double traces for the marathon

53 The comb for mane and tail is fitted to the strap which supports the traces of the "Cseklész" harness

54 Rope traces are mounted near to the straps for greater safety during the marathon

great strains account for its high popularity among Hungarian drivers.

The "Jukker" harness needs flat strap-traces. It is mainly used for training and cross-country driving, but is also quite suitable for dressage or obstacle driving.

Draught Harness

This is the simplest and cheapest harness on the market, and used mainly in agriculture and for the transportation of goods. In Hungary it is available ready-made in any shop for agricultural products.

Normally it has rope or chain traces. The neck-strap has been separated from the harness and is attached to the hook on the pole-end. Rings and buckles are made of black lacquered iron. Belt is placed under the soft pommel with stitched-on pommel-rings to absorb sweat.

This harness is very useful when breaking in young horses. Even a difficult horse cannot cause serious damage by tearing the harness apart or by creating situations in which the harness has to be cut. The draught harness is highly recommended for the training of foals and, after being recut, can be used also for general training.

Adjusting the Harness to the Horse

Let us consider the testing and adjusting of a made-to-measure harness. First the clips have to be buckled in a central position. Then the horses are led to the carriage. The determinant for adjusting the harness is the line of traction which changes position depending on the height of the double-tree.

For instance, if the horses are hitched into another carriage where the double-tree is situated lower than in the previous one, the line of traction will deflect, and if the double-tree is set higher than before, the buckle will loosen at that very point. The first situation is definitely more dangerous, because the pommel strongly presses against the horse's back chafing its skin. Therefore, it is advisable to have carriages with double-trees all at the same level. In winter, when making a horsedrawn sledge, the need to

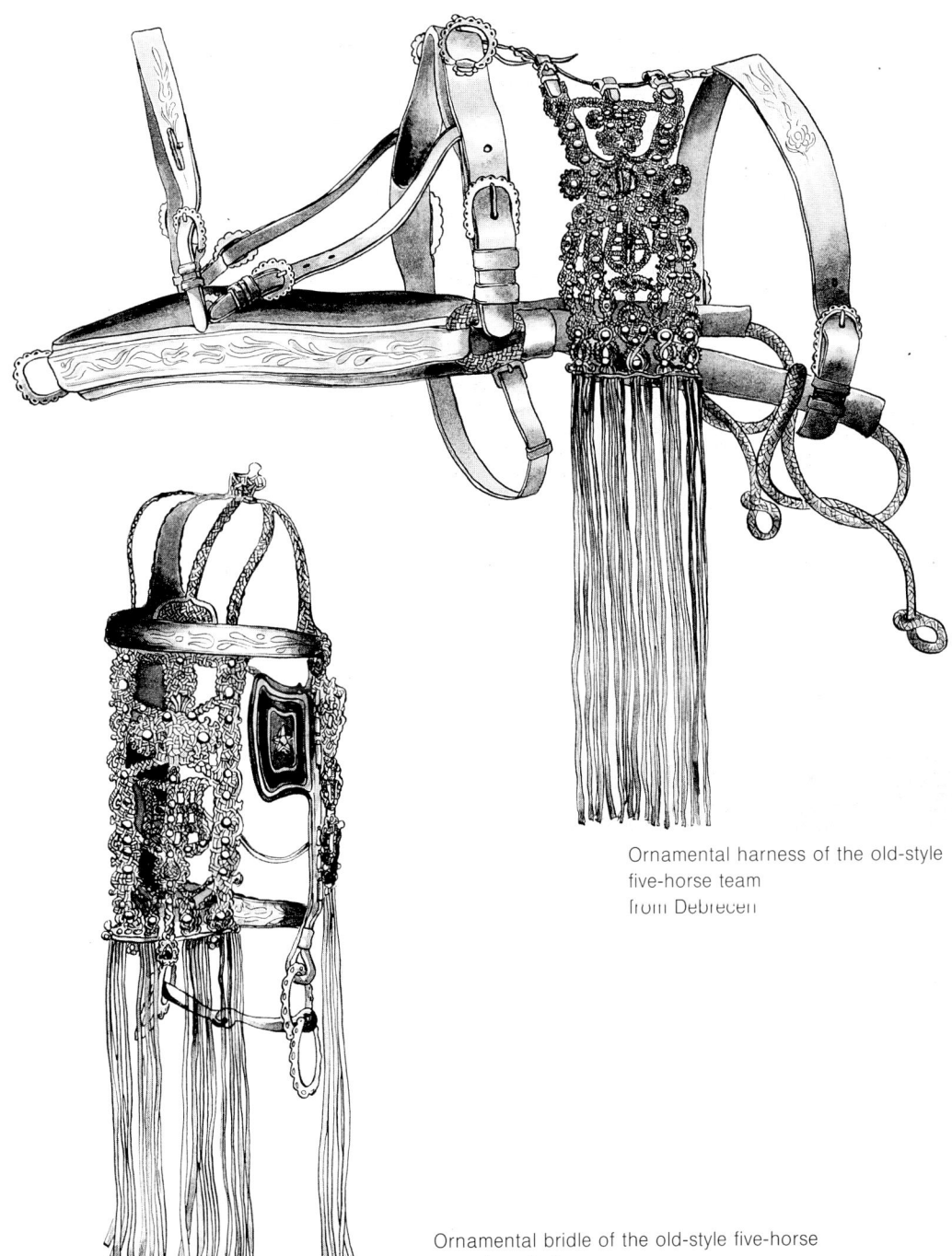

Ornamental harness of the old-style five-horse team from Debrecen

Ornamental bridle of the old-style five-horse team from Debrecen re-adjust the harness and to lengthen the traces of the wheelers should not be forgotten.

The line of traction should always be controlled from the ground-level while the horses are in action and the harness is being stretched.

To measure properly the correct length of the traces, the carriage should be in motion. If the wheelers are too close to the vehicle, they will probably kick the wheel or the double-tree. As this can happen only when at a rapid trot, the length of the traces should be checked while trotting. If the leaders are too near to the wheelers, the driver will soon become aware of this, as the latter will kick the former. This, too, can only be checked at an accelerated trot. The traces must not be too long either, for that lessens safe manœuvrability. Nowadays, every driver tries to make his team as short as possible, so that he can surmount narrow obstacles, especially in hairpin bends, more easily.

After the line of traction and the traces are correct, the reins should be adjusted according to the guide-lines in the related chapter.

There is no exact rule on how to carry out finer adjustments while driving (such as changing the bit), the driver has to develop a certain feeling for this and take prompt action.

55 "Jukker" harness. The racing four-in-hand of the Szilvásvárad Stud, drawn by Lipizaner stallions and driven by György Bárdos

56 Sledge-and-pair in the Bükk mountains. Driver: Lajos Debreceni with the Lipizaner team of the Szilvásvárad State Farm

The Driver's and the Groom's Dress

A very important and conspicuous characteristic of a Hungarian team is the outfit of the driver and the grooms (or other accompanying persons).

While the outfits have always kept up with fashion they incorporate many folk motifs.

Created on the large estates at the end of the last century, the outfits were similar in cut. Differences in ornamentation reflected the owner's financial status.

All but the richest peasantry wore another style of dress when they drove to a feast.

Both types of outfit have survived up until the present day.

The teams from the state farms established on the territory of large private estates after 1945 have preserved outfits typical of former times. The outfits worn by teams from the agricultural co-operatives which the small and middle peasants organized, continue to be in the folk-tradition. Both kinds of outfits have to be in accordance with the regulations set down for competitive events. However, gaudy, over-decorated costumes more suited to the operetta should be avoided; they tend to become grotesque parodies of the traditional.

The modern trend towards simplicity now allows both the driver and his assistant in a carriage-and-pair to appear in sporting attire. A four-in-hand with several grooms requires a more decorative appearance than a simple carriage-and-pair.

The main current requirement for carriages is to comply with the stipulations of competitions. The judging of the outlook of the team as a whole, in which not only the vehicle and the harness but also the dress of the driver and his assistants are assessed, does not feature in the points aggregate of teams as from 1987, yet outlook is a gesture to traditions. An important point of debate arises here; not only foreign judges, but even those from Hungary often do not know exactly to what degree national folklore motifs may decorate the dress of the driver and grooms, as these outfits should look neither too unadorned nor yet gaudy.

Hungarian competition-rules stipulate that Hungarian drivers must be dressed in sporting attire. This dress consists of a tailored jacket

57 The assistant driver of the team of the Tápiószentmárton Agricultural Co-operative in ceremonial coachman's livery

58 The assistant driver of the racing team of Kecskemét wears a ceremonial dress with a brimmed hat

The Driver's and the Groom's Dress

59 The competition four-in-hand of the Hortobágy State Farm. Driver: Gábor Fintha. The grooms in the traditional costume of the Hortobágy horse-herds

60 Blanket for the seat-box of the carriage of Szilvásvárad. Although, it is nicely decorated with Hungarian motifs, a *szűr* would suit it better

61 The grooms of László Juhász, champion in 1982, wear national costume

with a back slit, trouseres specially designed for riding, a suitable hat, a white shirt and a tie. This should be both smart and sporting.

As a carriage-driving competition is a formal event, dark clothing is considered appropriate to wear. It is very much in the driver's favour if his dress matches the colour of the covers and of the grooms' outfit. If the assistant driver wears national costume, the driver himself should be dressed in dark grey or black.

62 The rear decoration of the attire of an assistant driver. The team belongs to the Regöly Agricultural Co-operative

63 The assistant driver's ceremonial dress in the racing team of the Agricultural Complex of Mezőhegyes

The costume of the grooms and of the assistant drivers can be proper coachman's livery or the original national costume of a particular region of the country. The assistant driver of a carriage-and-pair may be attired in a sporting style similar to that of the driver.

Ceremonial dress is always close-fitting, the boots have a seam on the side, the shafts are stiff and the counters low. The characteristic broad-brimmed hat is adorned with ostrich feathers. A fringed silk tie and brown leather gloves complete the outfit.

Ceremonial dress is made of stout quality cloth which does not lose colour if wet or exposed to sunlight.

Some studs still have their own traditional dress. Bábolna has a livery of a basic green with gold braiding; Mezőhegyes has red with black braiding, and Szilvásvárad blue with richly gult braiding. The coachman's livery of Count István Széchenyi, a prominent personality in the Hungarian equestrian life of the last century, is also quite famous; it is dove-grey with black braiding. The orange-coloured Esterházy livery with black braiding and gold buttons is also well-known. The most attractive liveries are exhibited in the Hungarian Transport Museum and in the Agricultural Museum; and they influence the outfits of modern carriage-drivers.

A very important accessory to a coachman's clothing was the **szűr;** a long, loose-fitting, felt garment rather like a university gown with sleeves. It was worn like a cloak thrown over the shoulders and served as a raincoat. The long, wide collar of the **szűr** was an additional element decorating the coach. The modern covers for the seat-box are only poor imitations of this felt cloak, and carriage owners are advised to use an original.

There is not great call for winter attire these days, since carriage-driving events are always held in summer, but a few state studs do still have some for sleighing performances. Some characteristic articles of winter dress, such as fur-coats and fur-caps, are in the possession of the stud at Szilvásvárad.

National costume has always belonged to the carriages, as the majority of the vehicles are

64 Assistant drivers of the team of the Máriapócs Agricultural Co-operative in ceremonial coachman's livery

65 Folded *szűr* on the carriage's seat. It should be put on the seat of the assistant driver who is wearing a traditional costume or ceremonial dress. There is neither a *szűr* nor a blanket on the seat of the driver attired in sporting style

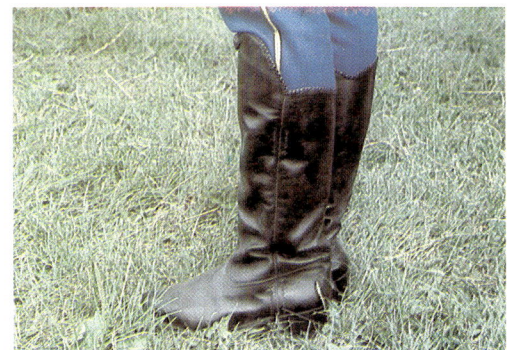

66 The boot, seamed on one side

The Driver's and the Groom's Dress

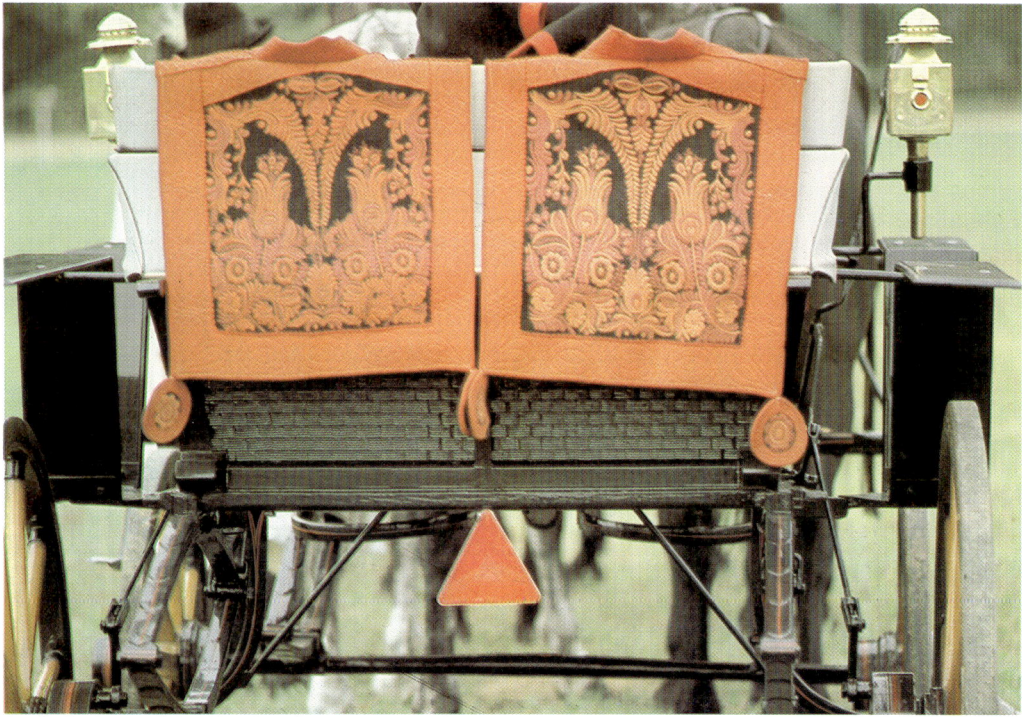

67 *Szűr* cloak of the Kecskemét team

68 *Szűr* cloak of the Dömsöd team

69 This blanket for the seat-box of the Dömsöd team is not Hungarian in style and may thus be criticized

rustic in style. Coaches for formal events used to be ornamented with ribbons and flowers, and the cushions on the seats to make them more comfortable had embroidered covers. The drivers of peasant's carts always had with them a **suba** which is a wide sheepskin coat reaching down to the heels, and of course, the **szűr** described above.

If the owner, whether an agricultural co-operative or state stud, is not to be represented, but the team itself chooses its own style, the dress of the team, harness and all other accessories should be matching in colour and style. The choice can be made from a great variety of national costumes, which do make events more colourful and interesting. However, care should be taken not to allow grooms to wear official livery on a rustic carriage and similarly, the grooms on a style carriage (e.g. "Esterházy", "Cziráky", "Károlyi") should not wear national costume.

If possible, the driver should select his assistants himself, thus ensuring the friendly atmosphere that makes for co-operation. Efficient collaboration, even at the preparatory stage, is half-way to success.

The Driver's and the Groom's Dress 53

Different Hungarian coachmen's coats (*szűrök*)
Szűr of the Kunság

Szűr from the region around Hajdúság and Debrecen

71 The blanket of the team of Állampuszta: not recommended for decoration; a *szűr* with the long, wide reverse would be better

70 An attractive cloak in Hungarian style on the carriage of Abádszalók

72 The emblem of the stud or of the club is to be found even on the blankets

54 The Driver's and the Groom's Dress

73 An assistant driver in the traditional costume of Bugac

74 The four-in-hand of the Nagycenk State Stud: Hungarian Half-Bred stallions hitched to a sledge. The assistant driver is wearing the traditional coachman's fur coat

The Technique of Hungarian Driving

While it is worth looking back to the traditional past of Hungarian carriage-driving for its own sake, it is interesting also because the Hungarian technique of driving has had success at all the most important world competitions. This technique, perfected over centuries, contains a valuable store of indispensable knowledge; and well-trained, reliable horses, correct and well-kept harness, decorative vehicle and national costumes are all to no effect without it.

The Proper Method of Holding and Using the Reins and the Whip

The Basic Grip

As mentioned previously, the frog on the reins should be adjusted so that it lies exactly in the driver's hands. The basic grip is to hold the reins by the frog in the left hand, while the nearside reins run between the little finger and the ring finger. Drivers with small hands should hold the reins immediately in front of the frog, while those with large hands are able to actually hold it.

On a Hungarian ornamental harness with patterned studs the saddler always makes the reins with buckles to match. Buckles with lacy patterns may be so sharp that they hurt the driver's hands and are often replaced by simple steel buckles covered with thin deerskin. This does not in any way clash with the style and will be accepted by the strictest of judges.

The basic grip is to hold the reins in the left hand and the whip in the right hand. Only when harnessing, unharnessing or waiting for a long period may the whip be placed in the whip-socket, which is mounted on the mudguard. This is a competition rule, and should be practised long before the event takes place.

The Actuating Grip

The reins are conveyed from the left hand to the ring and middle fingers of the right hand, and by pressing down the end of the thumb the reins are taken by the frog. Then the reins should be held raised, while keeping the distance between the two fists about 20 cm. The reason why the reins should be held in the right hand between the ring finger and middle finger is that the other fingers are necessary to hold the whip. The proper way of holding the whip is as follows: the whip-stock has to be aligned with the horse's left eye so that the stock-end points in the direction of the horse's ear.

When driving a carriage for the first time, it is of vital importance to learn how to change from the basic grip to the actuating grip, since all other grips are based on this. All the changes of grips have to be smooth so that the horses do not notice them. A beginner must practise until he can manage these changes automatically, i.e. without thinking about it.

The Basic Grip with the Whip in One's Hand

At the beginning of an event or at distribution of prizes, the driver has to salute by doffing his hat while driving onto the course. This gesture

75 Basic grip

76 Training a four-in-hand as seen from the driver's seat

77 Basic grip while the team is standing

The Technique of Hungarian Driving

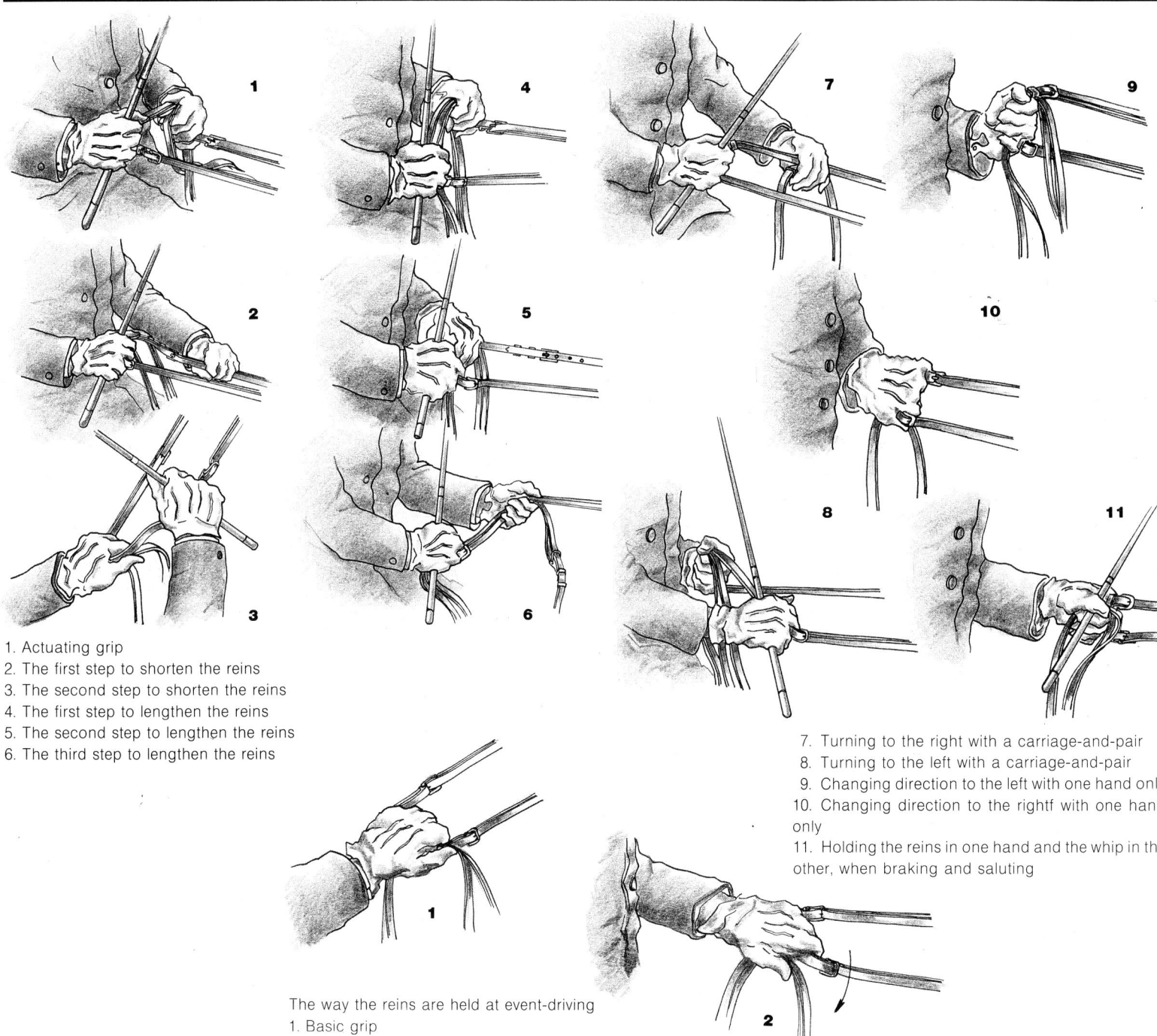

1. Actuating grip
2. The first step to shorten the reins
3. The second step to shorten the reins
4. The first step to lengthen the reins
5. The second step to lengthen the reins
6. The third step to lengthen the reins
7. Turning to the right with a carriage-and-pair
8. Turning to the left with a carriage-and-pair
9. Changing direction to the left with one hand only
10. Changing direction to the rightf with one hand only
11. Holding the reins in one hand and the whip in the other, when braking and saluting

The way the reins are held at event-driving
1. Basic grip
2. Basic grip and pulling the reins to the right

should be made with dignity and respect, and never hurriedly. The driver should take his hat off slowly, then hold it aside with the top upwards. He should then put it on again slowly and respectfully. This is very important, because the reins have to be held in the basic grip while saluting, and to leave the right hand free the whip should also be held in the left hand. It can be done by lifting the left forefinger, putting the whip-stock underneath and then pressing it down.

Some eventing teams are still equipped with handbrakes only. In order to be able to use them properly, the right hand has to be freed in the above-mentioned way.

Shortening the Reins

The reins have to be shortened to reduce speed, to halt and turn.

In the actuating grip both reins are in the left hand. The first step towards shortening them is to transfer both simultaneously to the right hand. To do this, the right hand slowly approaches the left hand until the right forefinger reaches the end of the near rein and presses it to the left rein. Then, the left hand slides forward on the near rein as far as it is necessary and then grasps it. The end of the near rein held by the right forefinger has to be released, and the shortened rein is finally taken over by the left hand. In this way the reins are held again in the basic grip but the driver has to change at once to the actuating grip by pulling both reins backward to give the horses the necessary instruction.

It cannot be stated in advance by how much the reins need to be shortened in certain situations. The driver has to develop a feeling for this during training.

Lengthening the Reins

The reins have to be lengthened to drive uphill or before changing the gait from trotting to pacing, so that the horses can lean forward while craning their necks.

The first step is exactly the same as that for shortening: the right hand approaches the left hand until the driver's forefinger reaches the end of the near rein and thus grasps it. Then the left hand slides backward on the rein as far as it is required, the left hand then clasps both reins for a second and the forefinger looses its hold of the rein. Then, by means of the right hand the off-rein should be helped into the left hand to take up the basic grip. Immediately after, the driver has to change over to the actuating grip.

In competitive driving, leading Hungarian carriage-drivers lengthen the reins in a different way: they begin as described above with both hands holding one rein-end but then they let the reins slide forward through their fingers as far as the horses need. This method requires only a short time provided the driver and horses harmonize perfectly. Beginners are advised to practise the classical way of lengthening.

Using the Reins when Turning

Hungarian carriages owe their success primarily to their manœuvrability, the decisive factor of which is the way the reins are held on the bends.

The proper technique of turning and using the reins is judged in dressage. Regulations for the marathon and for obstacle driving take into consideration only good results and not individual methods.

When turning right with a carriage-and-pair, the first thing to do is to shorten the reins slightly. Then the right hand should be lifted and the off-rein should be pulled towards the driver's left hip. At the same time the near rein should be loosened smoothly without any sudden motion. When turning left, the driver has to do exactly the opposite. If he sits on the right-hand side of the seat, he has to make an additional vigorous twist of the hand to turn properly. Nowadays, however, the driver's seat is mounted in the middle of the seat-box, so that the shortening and lengthening of the reins is the same procedure for both directions.

In dressage the teams have to describe a circle of a diameter of 30 m; the driver holding the reins in one hand. At first, the reins should be held in the basic grip. Circling to the left, the driver presses his fist towards his right hip and at the same time twists his fist so that his fingers are upward. Circling to the right, he pushes his fist away from his left hip and twists it outwards to the left. The whip is held in the right hand with the arm outstretched to the right at shoulder level.

Teams often have to make turns of 90° or complete circles. In a carriage-and-pair the driver then has to slightly shorten the reins, then catch hold of the rein on the turning side a little in front, before he pulls it backward. The other rein has to be loosened just as much as the horses need. Meanwhile, both fists have to be pressed into the opposite direction.

A four-in-hand makes a turn in compliance with the rules when, from a bird's eye view, the curve is approached cornerwise, and then the head of the inside wheeler is directed towards a point midway between the two leaders. It is the leaders in a four-in-hand which begin to turn by reacting to the shortening of the leading reins on the turning side.

When turning to the left with a four-in-hand the reins are held at first in the basic grip. Then both hands approach each other, palms down, until the forefinger and middle finger reach the end of the near rein. Both reins are then grasped vigorously by the right hand. The left hand is thus free, and the middle finger should be positioned between the driving rein of the saddle-horse (left wheeler) and that of the rein-horse (left leader).

The left hand can then slide forward as much as the bend makes necessary. The driving-rein of the left leader (rein-horse) should be grasped firmly and pulled backward as far as the frog, so that the middle finger hooked in the saddle-horse's rein should prevent the left hand from losing its hold and allow it to slide along the rein.

In dressage bends have to be taken cleanly and to make the wheelers turn properly, the driver has to counter the turn by simultaneously lifting and pulling his right fist towards his stomach with a twisting movement, so that the fingers are turned upward before the wheelers actually start turning.

At the very moment when the leaders have taken the bend and run straight ahead again, the driver has to release his left hand grip and loosen the off-leader's rein. The right hand stops the counter-check and the whole team is once again in the starting position.

If the team is not required to make a further turn soon after, the driver can return to the actuating grip, but if another bend is already in sight, the team should remain ready for it.

If the saddle-horse is a young, inexperienced animal and does not react properly to the driver's twisting hand-motion, or leans sideways in the bend, the driver should hook his left forefinger into the wheeler's rein while pulling the left leader's rein backward. This will pull the wheelers to the right. This drastic method should be applied only in training, as the wheelers of a well-trained four-in-hand should react to the already described counter-check.

When the four-in-hand turns to the right, the driver slightly shortens the reins and uses the basic grip. The middle finger of the right hand should be placed between the off-leader's rein and the wheeler's rein, then the right hand slides forward as much as the bend necessitates. Then the middle finger and the ring finger of the right hand tighten their grip on the off-leader's rein while pulling it gradually backward up to the frog. In the meantime, similarly to a left-handed bend, the other hand carries out the counter-check. For this, the left fist has to be simultaneously lifted, twisted and pulled towards the driver's stomach until all the fingers on the left hand are upward. After the turn has been completed, the leading rein in the right hand should be loosened and allowed to slide back to the starting position. The left hand gradually takes up the basic grip, and the team continues on the straight again.

Four-in-hands also have to be able to describe a circle 30 m in diameter. Before beginning to circle to the right, the leaders' driving rein on the turning side has to be slightly shortened, and pressed down by the thumb. The fist is pushed away and twisted in the same way as for a carriage-and-pair. When circling to the left, the shortened leading rein should be pressed vigorously between the little finger and the ring finger. The rest of the movements are as for a carriage-and-pair.

All these techniques need to be practised intensively to be able to make faultless turns. If

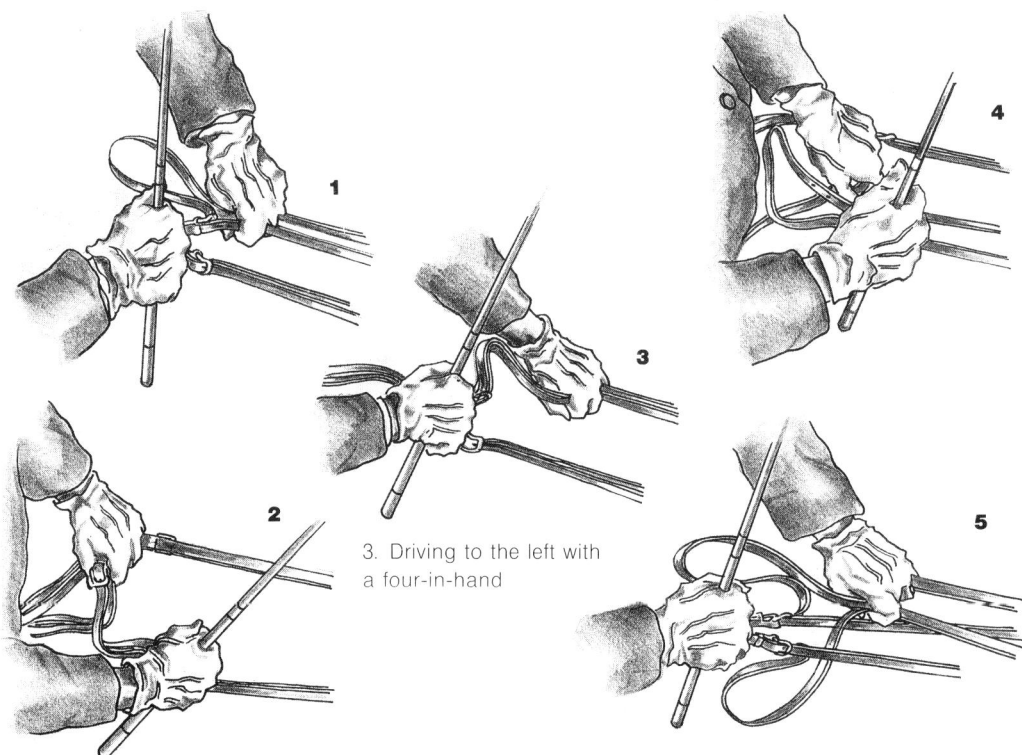

1. Driving to the right with a four-in-hand
2. Turning to the left with a four-in-hand
3. Driving to the left with a four-in-hand
4. Turning to the right with a four-in-hand
5. Bringing the horses to a halt

all the horses of a four-in-hand start to turn simultaneously, the whole team is very likely to turn over.

The driver has to be prepared long before the bend comes, as it takes time to place the fingers properly between the two reins. In marathon and obstacle driving there are no special stipulations concerning the reins. Thus many drivers keep their hands constantly between the two reins, in front of the frog. This method is very efficient when turning in any direction, as it eliminates a lot of the troublesome grips that cause a considerable loss of time.

Before the start of a marathon or an obstacle driving event, Hungarian race drivers buckle the frog two to three holes in front, so that they do not have to shorten the rein before making a bend. Undoubtedly, this method does not allow them to sit straight up and to hold their arms as prescribed, but they thus spare themselves two actions (shortening the reins and positioning their fingers) and so gain time.

These driving techniques have been created as natural consequences to the growing popularity and the official acceptance of carriage-driving as a sport, as well as to the increasing requirements of competitions and the inventive spirit of the drivers. If they had rigidly kept to the old methods, they would have never attained outstanding results.

Backing the Team

One phase of the dressage is the rein back. It is a most difficult task, and only a few teams are able to execute it correctly, i.e. on a straight line.

Before backing, the reins should be shortened and pulled firmly but lightly. If the horses react and back promptly, the reins can be loosened and then tightened again. These giving and taking actions of the reins should be repeated as long as the horses are required to back. Well-trained horses readily understand this language of the reins and back smoothly. One should never tug at the horse's mouth, if the animal refuses to back. An older horse may be in the team, which had not been taught to back or has been spoiled in some way. Such a horse should always be hitched together with another which is good at backing and, if possible, in a vehicle with stake braces, which is easy to hold straight.

If the team is to back on a sloping riverbank, it must halt first. The assistant driver should always have enough sugar cubes or oats with him to reward the horse. The first attempt at backing on a river-bank should be tried downhill, and then practised until the animals easily manage it without showing any signs of resistance.

The place where schooling is conducted should be frequently changed so that the horses do not become accustomed to one spot but concentrate on the tasks they have to fulfil. Once a horse is able to back downhill, the next step is to try backing on level ground and then to hitch it to a style-carriage. Having learned everything in all these situations, it can be put back into a four-in-hand.

The horse cannot be expected to learn everything in one day. The driver can be happy if the horse makes one step backward at all on the very first day. Never overdo the demand, otherwise the horse might refuse to obey. Backing should be practised for a maximum of ten minutes during training. The rest of the time should be used for other exercises. When backing, the driver should always shout exactly the same word of command so that the horses learn to obey at the sound of his voice.

Starting the Team

Before starting the driver holds the reins in the basic grip, then changes into the actuating grip. According to Hungarian tradition, the horses start on hearing the driver's voice. On the command to start, which is usually a short and cutting tone, the reins should be simultaneously shortened.

Sometimes the horses start when merely feeling the reins to be in the driver's hands, but this is not allowed at events, as, for instance, a guest may want to enter the carriage; and besides, it is not expected of a well-trained team. To teach the horses to start only on command, the driver first takes the reins in his hands and waits a few minutes before giving the command. Never forget to offer the horses some sugar cubes in the meantime.

Halting the Team

To halt the team the reins have to be shortened and pulled backwards while giving the command. If the team is trained well, the action of halting is smooth and spectacular. Moreover, the driver does not need to make much effort but simply has to give the sign to halt.

In dressage it is also necessary to demonstrate the ability to halt promptly when the team is at a brisk trot. The best way to teach this to the horses is to use a word of command.

If they obey on command in the marathon and in obstacle driving, it will be no problem to halt them at any time; which is impossible by merely pulling on the reins. Brakes can be used too, and foot-brakes are an advantage.

Changing Pace and Gait

In dressage the teams have to pace in two different ways; and to trot in three different ways: working trot, collected trot and extended trot. The main fault of most carriages is an inability to demonstrate clearly the different paces. As horses do learn these gaits easily, such weaknesses are the result of negligence on the part of the driver.

Changing gait and pace is brought about by loosening the reins and uttering a word of command at the same time. If the driver needs to use the whip, he must first take the reins in the basic grip to free his right hand. (The use of a whip, however, always incurs penalties.)

If we want the horse to walk after trotting or to move at a collected trot after some extended trotting, the tension of the reins has to be increased while calming the horses verbally. This slowing down may be assisted by foot-brakes; use of the hand-brake is prohibited in dressage.

In the marathon and obstacle driving the gallop is one of the accepted gaits. The gallop does not need much training, and it is a great help when the driver wants to change to a faster gait.

Using the Whip

Hungarian whips consist of two main parts: the whip-stock and the lash. Traditional Hungarian whips are quite easy to handle. The best whip-stocks available today are made of Manila-cane.

The whip-grip of a Hungarian ceremonial harness with notched studding can be ornamented with leather butterflies or fringes. It is very elegant, if the grip as a whole is covered with leather. In the presentation phase of an event, the judges always attach great importance to the whip-socket which should match the colour of the carriage.

The basic rule is moderation. Never whip the horse more than once and never hit it on the croup, but rather between the shoulders and the withers, as it may kick out.

The whip-stock should be neither too short nor too long. Experience shows that the most suitable whip for a carriage-and-pair is flexible and about 150 cm long, while the whip for a four-in-hand is a little more rigid and about 10 cm shorter. At the end of the whip-stock are two buttons separated by about 2 cm. The lash is bound between these two buttons. It is advisable to fit a small brass tube between the two buttons to help the lash to whirl unhampered round the stock. This kind of whip is not only very useful in a four-in-hand, but also in a carriage-and-pair.

The lash consists of the following parts, as found from the end of the whip-stock to the end of the lash: the base **(telek)**, the spindle, the waist, the cracker and the snapper.

The lash is generally made of leather but sometimes it is of cord painted black. Hungarian whips are characterized by their removable lashes and by the **telek** (on the base) which is a flat, double-tied, 20 cm long collar made of

The Technique of Hungarian Driving

Winding the whip-lash around the stock with a single movement

thin leather. On the one end of this **telek** there is a loop, through which the lash is fitted to the stock, and on the other end there is a rotating ring to which the waist is attached. The extension of the waist is, of course, the cracker. The snapper of braided raffia is bound to the end of the cracker, but it is used only in four-in-hands. Snapping and cracking the whip is a special Hungarian custom.

Present-day event-rules of the marathon and obstacle driving do allow the use of whips, although cracking them is quite unfamiliar to the English driving style. English curved whips do not even have a snapper on the end.

Older Hungarian drivers are of the opinion that the whip-lash in a carriage-and-pair has to be five hand-span between the end of the **telek** and the end of the snapper; i.e. the length of the lash is between 80 cm and 100 cm depending on the size of the driver's hand. The whip-lash of a four-in-hand should be about 250 to 300 cm.

Together with the stock this whip is long enough to reach as far as the leader horses. Some of the leading drivers use whips of 150 cm in the marathon and in obstacle driving.

This short whip has the advantage of not touching the ground, the driver can hold it open all the time as it cannot wind around the axles and it is therefore always ready for use. However, such a short whip should not be used in a four-in-hand for presentation, as it will certainly be penalized. Ornamentation, mostly leather fringes or "butterflies", is usually put on the top part of the waist, under the rotating ring. Hungarian whips are never decorated with colourful cotton tassels. As mentioned previously the whip must be held in the hand at all times. If the driver puts it down or loses it, his team will be disqualified. This is the reason why spare whips are allowed. Once the driver is accustomed to holding the whip all the time in his hand, even in training, it will not disturb him in handling the reins. The whip is held properly when the end of the stock points in the direction of the ear of one of the near-side horses in a carriage-and-pair, and towards the off-leader's ear in a four-in-hand.

Whips in a four-in-hand are held wound around the stock and are unwound before use, and wound up again afterwards.

This procedure requires a great deal of practice since the left hand is fully occupied holding the reins, i.e. the opening and closing of the whip has to be done with one hand. It is best to learn this from experienced drivers or from old coachmen.

Training Team Horses

Training of pure-breds begins at the age of three or three and a half years. The stud at Szilvásvárad has worked out a very efficient method of training foals for drawing carriages. It is well-known that the Szilvásvárad Lipizaner is rather stiff and sensitive, i.e. the training methods used there are suitable for all the other Hungarian breeds.

Foals marked for coaching should be selected in pairs according to colour and size. Fodder should be withheld for the first two weeks.

The training should begin on the longe when the horse is saddled. Two persons are usually needed for longeing, as an untrained animal probably refuses to walk in the given circle. Intelligent young animals learn quite quickly. A bridle without noseband, but with a foal-bit and halter are necessary for longeing. A foal should be tethered on both sides to the surcingle of the saddle. At Szilvásvárad in all the initial training the horses are saddled, and only later harnessed. Saddled horses develop contact with a human, react to the rein and to the aids conveyed through the bit and understand the commands more easily. Foals should always be talked to when longeing, starting and halting. Backing should be practised every day, later also in a team. When a foal already performs well on the longe, it should be ridden, while on the longe, by a light weight rider. Once it tolerates the rider and reacts properly to his aids, it should be ridden following a trained animal.

The longe should be buckled into the ring of the nose-brake which is fitted to the halting-bridle by a piece of ironwork, and never to the bit-ring. A very essential moment of the training is the mounting of the foal for the first time. The rider should be careful not to plop into the saddle as this can hurt and frighten the horse. Both the whip and sugar cubes are constant inducements. The whip should be used sparingly, it is sufficient to show it to the horse; but every good performance should be rewarded by sugar cubes.

Foals can be put in harness after three to four months of work with the saddle and longe. At first novices have to learn to draw a vehicle through being harnessed next to an older, well-schooled horse and once they can do this well, they can be hitched in pairs. Novices drawing a vehicle for the first time are nearly always frightened by the rattling noise. Therefore, they should be patted and calmed while being led. The first drives should be on quiet, peaceful non-macadamized roads, field paths or country lanes.

During the first two months the foals should walk and trot on even ground only, and halt and back occasionally.

Mostly a light carriage with stake braces and a simple draught harness are recommended for schooling.

Once foals properly haul stake-vehicles, understand the commands and react to the rein-aids, they can be hitched to style carriages. The bearing reins and the traces have to be adjusted rather loosely at first and tightened but lightly only after a few days. Turning should be practised in a style carriage. After having driven around for about 4 to 5 km in the countryside, the team can drive on a course and practise how to change pace, to halt, to back, and to trace a figure of eight. This method will make nearly every foal into a useful carriage-horse. At Szilvásvárad several hundred foals have been trained without any accidents using this method.

Only calm, well-balanced, i.e. even-tempered persons who are patient and have a vocation for this kind of work should train foals.

In putting together a four-in-hand, the main point is that the wheelers should be strong, calm and reliable animals, while the leaders should be manœuvrable, agile and not shy.

How to Prepare a Team for Competitions

Carriage-driving competitions last three days. On the first day there is presentation and dressage, on the second day the marathon, and on the third day the obstacle driving. It is a very complex challenge, which requires much knowledge, attention and training.

Presentation and Dressage

Until 1987 these were separate events, and both belonged to the first day, and so they were registered as A/I. and A/II. Both winners were awarded separate prizes.

The presentation is actually a kind of "beauty contest" in which a three-member jury judges the competing teams.

A very essential aspect is that the horses of a team should be uniform in colour and size. The harness should be put on correctly and the team has to be fully equipped.

The driver and the grooms should be dressed according to the rules. All the parts of the

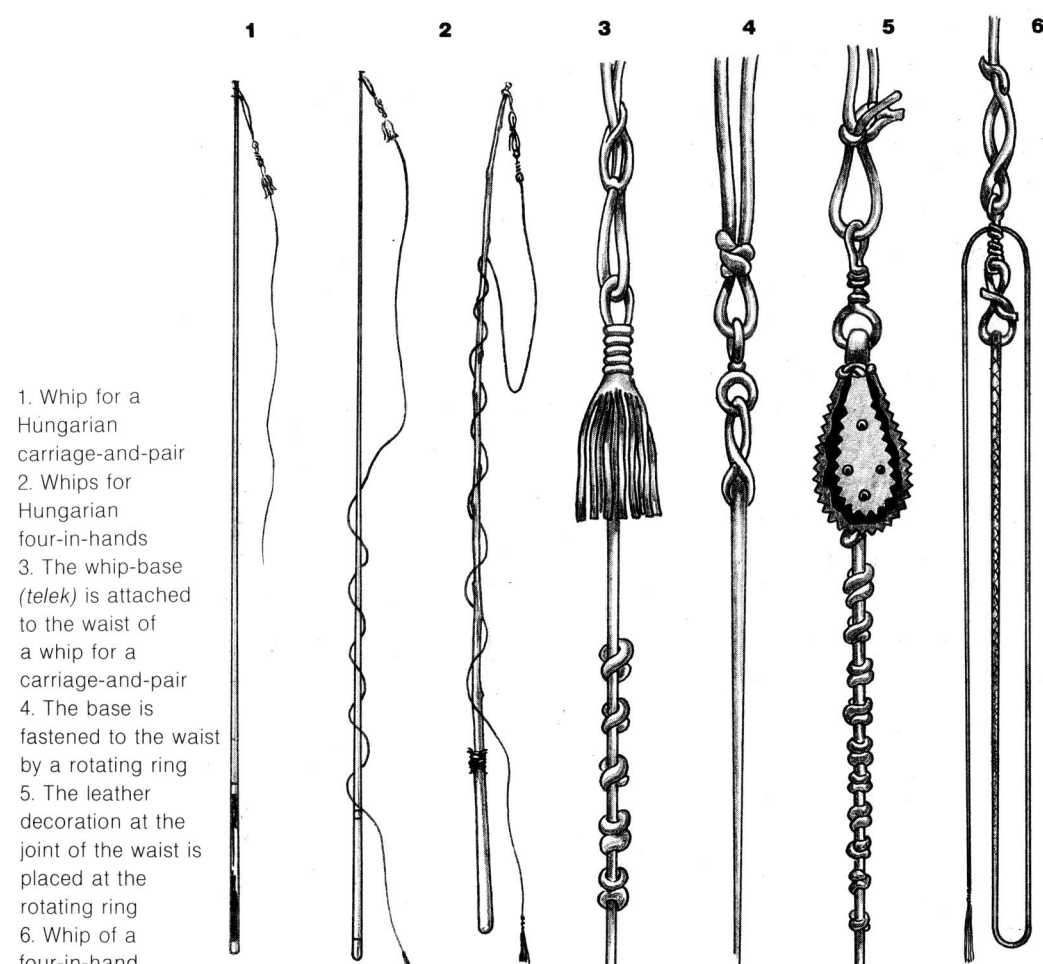

1. Whip for a Hungarian carriage-and-pair
2. Whips for Hungarian four-in-hands
3. The whip-base (telek) is attached to the waist of a whip for a carriage-and-pair
4. The base is fastened to the waist by a rotating ring
5. The leather decoration at the joint of the waist is placed at the rotating ring
6. Whip of a four-in-hand

78 Daily training at Bugac

carriage and accessories (shabracks, blankets, upholstery, dress) should co-ordinate in colour and style.

Further points are awarded according to the trimness of the team, i.e. the horses, harness, carriage, dress, boots and shoes should all be in the best condition. Axle grease may drip or the expensive, stylish boots of the grooms can be dusty. On the harness, mainly the trimness of the studding and of the brass terrets are most likely to be criticized. It is not sufficient to merely wipe the brass just before the event, as the green oxide layer is not so easy to remove.

A minor fault is when the candles in the lamps droop because of the heat. This can be prevented by using very short candles of about 1 to 1,5 cm, so that they are not pressed by the spring fixing the lamp. A team with clumsy, rashly-made brake-blocks "decorated" on the slipper side with pieces cut from a tractor-tyre suggests very careless preparatory work.

Although since 1987 A/I. has only been considered in the points aggregate, below we describe it for two reasons. First, the outlook of the carriage should always be immaculate, second, the rules can be subject to change in the future.

The grooms play a very important role in this part of the event, since it is the result of their daily tasks of maintaining the harness and vehicle which is to be judged.

It is very important to know how and where to store the equipment. The best storage place is a cupboard which can be securely closed and, if possible, with a glass door. This cupboard should not be in the stable itself, because the ammoniac fumes damage the leather and metal fittings of the harness. Similar considerations apply to the storing of the carriage.

The best method of transporting the harness to an event is to put it in a chest specially adapted to allow the harness to be correctly hung and not simply laid inside. Such chests made of pinewood (deal) and wood-fibre board are the easiest to move and carry. Transporting the harness in a simple case is not expedient as some parts of it may crease or break. Also putting all the pieces into the case and unpacking them consumes a great deal of time. Any part of a harness hung up in a special chest can be taken out quickly and easily.

The second part on the first day is the dressage. (Event A/II.)

Four-in-hands have to perform within a quadrangle measuring 40 m by 100 m. The dressage programme is designed to show whether the driver and the horses fully co-ordinate or not. If not, the team will not be able to execute correctly the different tasks set. All the exercises should be practised separately during training hours until the team performs perfectly. Since there are not two horses which are sensitive to the same degree, every horse, even sisters and brothers or those of one breed, reacts differently to the aids conveyed by means of the rein, the voice and the whip.

Training should always be preceded by some introductory work, since horses saturated by stable-fumes are not able to concentrate on the driver, and they may start to run, play or just refuse to obey, even in a well-trained team.

Setting off from the stable, the horses should first walk for 1 km and never trot. The trot is the second gait which, if possible, should be on a country-road for a distance of 3 to 4 km. This work should be enough to rid the horses of the stable-fumes. On the way to the training course the team should alternately pace and trot, halt and back, as well as change pace and move at a collected trot, at a working trot and at an extended trot. Training can start when the team reaches the course. It is not advisable to go

How to Prepare a Team for Competitions

79 Correct greeting. Ferenc Muity with the team of the Kecskemét State Farm

80 György Bárdos before leading his team forward for presentation

through the whole programme beforehand, because the horses learn the sequence of the exercises by heart and then, at the event, they may anticipate a turn earlier than necessary.

Such independent actions can have unfortunate consequences. For instance, the horse, but not the driver intends to turn and the result is an ugly struggle which, of course, is at once noticed by the judges. All the individual figures of the dressage should, therefore, be practised separately and the programme as a whole exercised only once or twice a week. The circles should always be varied, the best is to trace a figure of eight. If the horses lose elan while circling, the pace should be changed: from a collected trot to a working trot, then an extended trot, and back down to collected trot. Halting and backing should be practised in between.

After these fast gaits the horses should be made to walk again. Lively, sensitive horses should be calmed down. If necessary, the groom should dismount from the carriage, pat the horses and offer them sugar cubes while the team is slowly walking. Once the horses are walking calmly but energetically, the driver can take all the reins in one hand and try to drive slalom.

No exercise should be practised for so long that it becomes boring, the horses should always be animated so that they concentrate on the driver. If they fail to carry out a task, they should not be forced to repeat it, but allowed to try it again later. In nearly every four-in-hand there is a horse which reacts too sensitively, i.e. walks too slowly and then breaks into a fast trot. This kind of horse, if it is capable and has a good gait, is worth special attention. It should first be trained on the longe, then saddled and finally harnessed next to a well-schooled animal which is also not too phlegmatic.

81–83 Preparing the team for presentation.
1. Action: mounting the whipple-tree and putting the blankets, whip and reins in place

2. Action: first the two wheelers are led out of the stable. Then the bearing rein has to be buckled in and the reins put on properly

3. Action: after the wheelers the leaders are hitched to the vehicle. First the connecting strap is buckled in, then the reins and the traces are mounted

The Technique of Hungarian Driving

84 György Bárdos during dressage

85 Marathon on the sodden plain of Hortobágy

86 Hungarian Half-Bred four-in-hand of the Állampuszta Farm at the marathon

Before driving, these sensitive horses should be limbered up to avoid their disturbing the others. On the day of the event special care must be taken of these horses; they should be run in already at early dawn to leave time to dry and rub down afterwards.

During competition the driver must wear gloves, and therefore, they should be worn for training in order to become accustomed to them. Posture is another vital question in both training and eventing; the driver should always sit straight up.

The reins should be adjusted beforehand at a collected trot and in the actuating grip so that the frogs lie in the driver's hand or behind it.

Once the competition has started, there is no time for experiment. The preadjustment will not damage the reins, but give the driver a feeling of security and save him unnecessary nervousness.

Daily training is essential if dressage is to be successful.

Cross-Country Driving or the Marathon

To meet the demands of the marathon, the team should be manœuvrable and enduring, i.e. having the necessary stamina and staying power. The distance to be covered is between 20 and 30 km on very different kinds of road: loose sand, gravel, loess or plain, hilly and rocky ground and sometimes even in the mountains.

The competition-rules do not include any stipulation concerning soil conditions, and in rainy weather driving is of course, even more difficult. The complete distance is divided into five sections:

A — collected trot............................6–15 km
B — walk... 1–1.1 km
C — extended trot...........................3 km
D — walk...1–1.1 km
E — obstacle driving.......................6–10 km

This shows clearly that there are two walking sections, i.e. only those teams which are able to walk at a lively and steady pace can gain good

87 Carriage-and-pair at the marathon. Driver: Erika Szabó

88 Carriage-and-pair at the marathon. Driver: Mihály Fehér with the team of Apajpuszta

89 Carriage-and-pair at the marathon

The incorrect and correct methods of turning a carriage-and-pair

The false and the correct way of turning a four-in-hand

results. To practise the extended pace it is best to make the team walk downhill every day. If the training course is on even ground, the team should walk either on loose sand or on rather soft ground. Of the breeds in Hungary, it is only the pure-blood Arab which, because of its physique, cannot meet the requirements of the average time for walking.

The first section at a trot (A) usually does not raise difficulties. Teams which are fit manage it easily. The set distance has to be covered within a given time, therefore the assistant driver should always use a stop-watch, even in training. It is not easy to assess the time passing without a watch when driving on country-roads and paths.

To keep the horses fit, they should be driven 30 to 40 km daily, and this should include dressage. László Kruckió, director of the Apajpuszta stud, worked out an excellent method to prepare his horses for exhausting competitions over a distance of 100 km. He had the horses swim in irrigation-canals. This did not weaken the horses' legs, but just the contrary; the muscles, heart and lungs were strengthened. A further advantage of swimming is that no dilation of the tendon sheaths develops on the horses' legs, and moreover, any existing problems of this kind may even be cured by this method. Although, present-day competitions do not take place over a distance of 100 km, regular swimming exercise is recommended.

The daily training should begin with a preliminary cross-country drive, in the course of which difficult obstacles should be avoided as far as possible. However, on coming across a brook or a ditch, the driver should not hesitate to pass through. Only after the horses have been limbered up to be supple enough for dressage, should the more complicated obstacles be attempted. When this stage is reached, the horses are then able to concentrate fully on the rein-aids and on the commands. It would be of advantage to construct a special course with variable obstacles for cross-country driving near the dressage-course, where the team can train two or three times a week. The order and approach to how the obstacles are tackled should be varied from time to time, so that the

90 Forest marathon

91 Obstacle with barrels. Driver: Mihály Bálint with the four-in-hand of Kiskunfélegyháza

The Technique of Hungarian Driving

92 Competition four-in-hand of the State Farm of Kecskemét. Driver: Ferenc Muity

93 Competition four-in-hand from the Dózsa Agricultural Co-operative of Dömsöd

94 A cadre obstacle of the marathon: the sand pit

horses do not get bored. Only when the team has executed one task satisfactorily, should another be attempted.

Carriage-driving competitions always have some typical, "cadre" obstacles to be passed in more or less the same way each time. For instance a curved narrow path composed of wood-logs requires the teams to describe serpentines or figures of eight. A quite popular alternative is the run between barrels. Nearly every marathon course contains a water-filled ditch, and so the horses should practise as much as possible passing through such ditches without hesitation. If they have an aversion to

95 Marathon obstacle at Hortobágy. Driver: György Bárdos with the racing team from the Lipizaner Stud of Szilvásvárad

96 In the mountains of Szilvásvárad. Driver: Mihály Bálint with the four-in-hand of Kiskunfélegyháza

97 Every competitive event must have a water obstacle. Driver: Gábor Fintha

98 Driving event for carriage-and-pair. The narrow marathon obstacle known as the "Hamburg star"

water, they should be led first in pairs into the shallow and then into deeper water. Once the pairs are no longer shy at the water the four-in-hand may try it. Care must be taken not to frighten the horses, and not to create any association of fear or punishment by beating. Therefore, the whip should be used only if there is absolutely no other alternative. When the horses have stepped into the water, use of the whip should stop at once. When the weather is so dry that there is no water in the ditches, the teams can be trained by driving over a nylon sheet spread out on the ground. Teams which do not hesitate to pass over a nylon sheet will not be afraid of water.

The extended trot (Section C) has been introduced for the marathon in the last few years. Hungarian teams usually have no problem in keeping within the time limits, but, nonetheless, they should still trot at speed and be timed once or twice a week.

Training should be ended with a slow walk until the animals are dry.

There is always a breathing space between sections, but the teams should not be halted, as the horses will become stiff.

Once the event is over, the teams should walk about for half-an-hour or so. Before tethering the horses in the stall, all their legs should be washed, and all parts of the body which have been covered by the harness should be curried till dry.

99 Snapshot of the marathon. Driver: László Juhász

100 Marathon. The obstacle is a water-ditch in the forest. Driver: Gábor Fintha

The Technique of Hungarian Driving

101 Marathon obstacle on the Hortobágy plain. Driver: György Bárdos with the racing team from the Lipizaner Stud of Szilvásvárad

102 A frequent marathon obstacle is that of driving between wood-piles. Driver: Sándor Krizsán with the four-in-hand from Mezőhegyes

Obstacle Driving

The course for obstacle driving is either on turf or in a stadium. The obstacles to be negotiated in the sequence are: gates, corner turns, U or Z-formed passages and there are sometimes water-ditches and platforms. Obstacles requiring the teams to back have been eliminated by the international regulations. The gates are 30 or 40 cm wider than the distance between the wheels of the carriages, which is measured exactly before the competition starts. The gates are made of plastic according to an international pattern. A ball is placed on top of each marker and if this ball falls down, the team is given a penalty point. Omitting an obstacle or leaving the penalty zone before completing the obstacle also incurs penalty points. Disqualification is involved if the team takes the wrong course.

The rather spectacular nature of obstacle driving gives it a high entertainment rating, and it usually attracts several thousand spectators. It is important to be prepared for this, as no driver is without nerves. Some drivers have the temperament to deal easily with the presence of large numbers of spectators, others tend to become over-excited. Beginners should try to ignore the spectators and to concentrate on their team's peformance.

Training for obstacle driving can be carried out together with that for dressage. It is advisable to vary the size and types of gate used in training in order to avoid surprises during events. Only when a team manages to turn easily, should driving between gates start.

As obstacle driving is the last section of the event, the horses generally come to it quite tired and stiff. Introductory work should limber them up and make them alert. As they will have worked hard at the marathon on the previous day there is no need to fear the effect of stable-fumes. They will need a lot of walking, changing pace and turning to take out the stiffness and show their suppleness.

The same harness should be used for obstacle

103 "Székely" gate as an obstacle

104 Various ingenious obstacles await the teams at obstacle driving. Driver: Sándor Krizsán

How to Prepare a Team for Competitions

105 László Juhász approaching the finish of the obstacle driving

106 Driving through the gates at a gallop. Driver: Sándor Krizsán

107 Obstacle driving, water-ditch

108 Successful rectangular turn. Driver: László Juhász with the competition four-in-hand of Kiskunfélegyháza

109 To negotiate correctly between the gates at obstacle driving needs a lot of practice

driving as for dressage. The newest regulations allow harness without decoration of the bridle and sides, but as the regulations are always open to change, training with ornamental harness is recommended, but not, of course, with expensive braided fringes. Simple fringes with openwork will do for training. The main point is that the horses should get accustomed to wearing them.

Before obstacle driving starts, the frogs on the reins should be buckled further forward, just as they were before the marathon. A four-in-hand should be as short and narrow as possible. The swingle-trees should be pushed towards the pole, and the connecting straps buckled short. The leaders' traces should also be short but not so short that the wheelers would kick the leaders' legs. In obstacle driving the leaders do not have to pull, and so their reins may be buckled back one to two holes at the frog. A team which is not held closely together is handicapped. All this suggests that drivers should adjust the harness and the holes on the reins beforehand when training.

In a similar way, an inside point on the double-tree should be taken to which the holding straps of the swingle-tree can be fastened before obstacle driving, so that the wheelers are forced to come closer to each other.

*

We are confident that this comprehensive survey on carriage-driving in Hungary will be of use to both present and future carriage-racing drivers and to everyone with an interest in this sport.

110 Obstacle driving. Driver: Géza Abonyi of Kiskunfélegyháza

112 Z-shaped obstacle. Driver: Sándor Fülöp

111 Gábor Fintha obstacle driving. One can clearly see that the leaders' traces are hanging down, so that the animals are not pulling the vehicle. The team is easily manœuvrable in obstacle driving

Score Sheets

Results of European Driving Championships: Four-In-Hand

1971 Budapest
1. I. Abonyi (Hungary)
2. S. Fülöp (Hungary)
3. J. Papp (Hungary)
   Teams:
1. Hungary
2. FRG
3. Poland

1973 Windsor
1. A. Dubey (Switzerland)
2. L. Dondin (Switzerland)
3. Nicholson (GB)
   Teams:
1. Switzerland
2. FRG
3. Great Britain

1975 Sopot
1. I. Abonyi (Hungary)
2. Gy. Bárdos (Hungary)
3. F. Muity (Hungary)
   Teams:
1. Hungary
2. Poland
3. FRG

1977 Donaueschingen
1. Gy. Bárdos (Hungary)
2. T. Velstra (Netherlands)
3. E. Jung (FRG)
   Teams:
1. Hungary
2. Poland
3. FRG

1979 Haras du Pin
1. Gy. Bárdos (Hungary)
2. M. Bálint (Hungary)
3. S. Walisewski (Poland)
   Teams:
1. Hungary
2. Great Britain
3. Poland

1981 Zug
1. Gy. Bárdos (Hungary)
2. G. Bowman (GB)
3. Adamczak (Poland)
   Teams:
1. Hungary
2. Poland
3. Great Britain

Results of Driving World Championships: Four-In-Hand

1972 Münster
1. A. Dubey (Switzerland)
2. F. Müller (FRG)
3. Nicolson (Switzerland)
   Teams:
1. Great Britain
2. Switzerland
3. FRG

1974 Frauenfeld
1. S. Fülöp (Hungary)
2. C. Iseli (Switzerland)
3. G. Bowman (GB)
   Teams:
1. Great Britain
2. Switzerland
3. Poland

1976 Apeldoorn
1. I. Abonyi (Hungary)
2. E. Jung (FRG)
3. S. Walisewski (Poland)
   Teams:
1. Hungary
2. FRG
3. Poland

1978 Kecskemét
1. Gy. Bárdos (Hungary)
2. S. Fülöp (Hungary)
3. F. Muity (Hungary)
   Teams:
1. Hungary
2. FRG
3. Great Britain

1980 Windsor
1. Gy. Bárdos (Hungary)
2. G. Bowman (GB)
3. T. Velstra (Netherlands)
   Teams:
1. Great Britain
2. Hungary
3. Poland

1982 Apeldoorn
1. T. Velstra (Netherlands)
2. Gy. Bárdos (Hungary)
3. L. Juhász (Hungary)
   Teams:
1. Netherlands
2. Hungary
3. Great Britain

1984 Szilvásvárad
1. L. Juhász (Hungary)
2. Gy. Bárdos (Hungary)
3. M. Bálint (Hungary)

Teams:
1. Hungary
2. Sweden
3. Great Britain

1986 Ascot
1. T. Velstra (Netherlands)
2. I. Chardon (Netherlands)
3. L. Juhász (Hungary)
   Teams:
1. Netherlands
2. Hungary
3. FRG

1988 Apeldoorn
1. I. Chardon (Netherlands)
2. C. Pahlsson (Sweden)
3. J. Bozsik (Hungary)
   Teams:
1. Netherlands
2. Hungary
3. FRG

Danube-Alpine Cup: Carriage-and-Pairs

1979 Luxembourg
1. W. Stilhart (Switzerland)
   Teams:
1. Switzerland

1980 Fraunfeld
1. József Bozsik (Hungary)
   Teams:
1. Hungary

1981 Kecel
1. József Bozsik (Hungary)
   Teams:
1. Hungary

1982 Nördlingen
1. István Fehér (Hungary)
   Teams:
1. Hungary

1983 Rome
1. M. R. Pieper (FRG)
   Teams:
1. FRG

1985 Laxenburg
1. Merk Meiner (Switzerland)
   Teams:
1. Switzerland

1986 Oberriet
1. Artur Langg (Switzerland)
   Teams
1. Switzerland